THE LITTLE BOOK OF

Police Youth Dialogue

THE LITTLE BOOKS OF JUSTICE & PEACEBUILDING

Published titles include:

The Little Book of Restorative Justice: Revised & Updated, by Howard Zehr
The Little Book of Conflict Transformation, by John Paul Lederach
The Little Book of Family Group Conferences, New-Zealand Style, by Allan MacRae and Howard Zehr
The Little Book of Strategic Peacebuilding, by Lisa Schirch
The Little Book of Strategic Negotiation, by Jayne Seminare Docherty
The Little Book of Circle Processes, by Kay Pranis
The Little Book of Contemplative Photography, by Howard Zehr
The Little Book of Restorative Discipline for Schools, by Lorraine Stutzman Amstutz and Judy H. Mullet
The Little Book of Trauma Healing, by Carolyn Yoder
The Little Book of Biblical Justice, by Chris Marshall
The Little Book of Restorative Justice for People in Prison, by Barb Toews
The Little Book of Cool Tools for Hot Topics, by Ron Kraybill and Evelyn Wright
El Pequeño Libro de Justicia Restaurativa, by Howard Zehr
The Little Book of Dialogue for Difficult Subjects, by Lisa Schirch and David Campt
The Little Book of Victim Offender Conferencing, by Lorraine Stutzman Amstutz
The Little Book of Restorative Justice for Colleges and Universities, by David R. Karp
The Little Book of Restorative Justice for Sexual Abuse, by Judah Oudshoorn with Michelle Jackett and Lorraine Stutzman Amstutz
The Big Book of Restorative Justice: Four Classic Justice & Peacebuilding Books in One Volume, by Howard Zehr, Lorraine Stutzman Amstutz, Allan MacRae, and Kay Pranis
The Little Book of Transformative Community Conferencing, by David Anderson Hooker
The Little Book of Restorative Justice in Education, by Katherine Evans and Dorothy Vaandering
The Little Book of Restorative Justice for Older Adults, by Julie Friesen and Wendy Meek
The Little Book of Race and Restorative Justice, by Fania E. Davis
The Little Book of Racial Healing, by Thomas Norman DeWolf, Jodie Geddes
The Little Book of Restorative Teaching Tools, by Lindsey Pointer, Kathleen McGoey, and Haley Farrar

The Little Books of Justice & Peacebuilding present, in highly accessible form, key concepts and practices from the fields of restorative justice, conflict transformation, and peacebuilding. Written by leaders in these fields, they are designed for practitioners, students, and anyone interested in justice, peace, and conflict resolution.

The Little Books of Justice & Peacebuilding series is a cooperative effort between the Center for Justice and Peacebuilding of Eastern Mennonite University and publisher Good Books.

THE LITTLE BOOK OF

Police Youth Dialogue

A Restorative Path Toward Justice

DR. MICAH E. JOHNSON AND JEFFREY WEISBERG

Good Books®

New York, New York

Good Books books may be purchased in bulk at special discounts for sales promotion, corporate gifts, fund-raising, or educational purposes. Special editions can also be created to specifications. For details, contact the Special Sales Department, Good Books, 207 West 36th Street, 11th Floor, New York, NY 10018 or info@skyhorsepublishing.com.

Good Books is an imprint of Skyhorse Publishing, Inc.®, a Delaware corporation.

Visit our website at www.goodbooks.com

10 9 8 7 6 5 4 3 2 1

Library of Congress Cataloging-in-Publication Data is available on file.

Print ISBN: 978-1-68099-708-8
eBook ISBN: 978-1-68099-731-6

Series editor: Barbara Toews
Cover photograph: Howard Zehr

Printed in the United States of America

Contents

1
The Takers

Takers. Heavily armed tyrants invaded communities to terrorize and take loved ones away. Mike-Mike was born in Eatonville, Florida into an African American family. The first time Mike-Mike ever saw a police officer in person was when they came to take his father away to jail. The second time he ever saw a police officer, they came to take seven-year-old Mike-Mike away from his grandparents to live with his estranged mother. Mike-Mike thought to himself, *if they can steal me away from my family, these takers can do anything they want*. Weeks later, they took his father away again, this time for three years. Mike-Mike learned to write through drafting letters to his father in prison. Throughout his childhood, Mike-Mike's family lived in impoverished neighborhoods that were frequently targeted by police. As he grew up, he came to feel as if community members were being hunted by these Takers dressed as police officers. They would appear unannounced on his block and even at school to interrogate, terrorize, and take with impunity. The year he turned eleven, Mike-Mike himself suddenly became a target. Anytime he saw a police officer, they interrogated him as a criminal and searched his belongings. This occurred weekly. Even the most respected adults and elders in the community were afraid and powerless.

Mike-Mike began running whenever he saw a badge, a gun, or a uniform, heard sirens, or saw any signs of law enforcement. If he was unable to run, he put his hands in the air and remained as silent as possible, quietly praying that he would survive the Takers. At twelve, he was arrested, handcuffed, and taken to a juvenile detention facility because officers suspected he was truant, and his under-resourced school, which kept poor attendance records, confused his records with another student's. Two years later, Mike-Mike was riding in the back seat of a car that was pulled over by the police. The police ordered Mike-Mike and his friends out of the car and aggressively shoved them onto the concrete on the side of the road, screaming and cursing orders at them. Mike-Mike had witnessed this routine many times, but somehow he mustered the courage to ask, "Why are you doing this to us? What did we do wrong?" They threatened to kick out his teeth if he did not shut his mouth and ordered him to stare at the ground. His friends fearfully whispered to him to be quiet. Say nothing. Do nothing. Mike-Mike obeyed. They laid there for an hour, handcuffed as the entire city, it seemed, drove by and stared at them. They were humiliated and traumatized. They were all linemen on the high school football team, and Mike-Mike had just made the honor roll for academic excellence. Their talent, character, and achievements could not shield them from these run-of-the-mill violent, traumatic, and potentially fatal encounters with law enforcement.

One day, when the police conducted their routine interrogation and search of the youth in his community, Mike-Mike's brother protested their harassment. As a result, he was slammed on the hood of their car and arrested. Mike-Mike ran to the phone inside the house and dialed 911. He pleaded, "Can you please help us? Every day these cops come to our block and mess with us. They took my brother, and I think they will hurt him. Can you please send the real police to come help us?" The voice on the other end of the phone promised to help and ended the call. Mike-Mike peeked through the blinds waiting for the arrival of the good cops. He imagined that a more experienced, highly trained, and friendly police unit would arrive and passionately defend them against the bad cops who tormented their childhoods. Moments later, the phone rang. The same voice said, "The police officer that arrested your brother is outside your house and he wants to speak to you. Can you go outside to talk with him?" *Wow!*, he thought to himself. *Everyone is in on it. There is no such thing as a good cop, and there are no heroes in blue coming to defend us. She sounded so nice,* Mike-Mike thought, *but even she wanted the officer to see my face so he could take revenge. At best, he will use his status to sway the conversation in a way that continues the bullying by powerful police and the abuse of defenseless youth.* Even as a teenager, Mike-Mike knew there was no conversation that would change a lifetime tradition of police bullying his family and community. He was certain then more than ever that it was not safe to step one foot outside until the streets were clear of all police officers. He continued to avoid police whenever possible. When they caught him and interrogated him, he lied or remained silent.

He would never help them. They had been the arch nemeses of his community his entire life.

Mike-Mike's attempt to call the police on the police encapsulates the emotions and experiences of Black youth across the nation. His encounters with law enforcement were characterized by persecution, aggression, and loss, yet he wanted desperately to believe in officers he could trust and turn to for protection. Most Black, indigenous, and people of color (BIPOC) have stories of their own traumatic encounters with police, which are further compounded by national news stories of police violence and brutality. Over and over, BIPOC have seen people who look like them, their brothers or sisters, fathers or mothers, sons or daughters, shot and killed at the hands of police or other agents of authority. It has been eight years since Trayvon Martin's death in 2012 and George Zimmerman's subsequent acquittal that ignited the Black Lives Matter movement, but police community relations have not improved and for BIPOC youth, the American nightmare[1] is ongoing. The litany of BIPOC lives lost to police violence has only grown. In 2020, the realities of anti-Black racism and police brutality are ever present in the killings of Ahmaud Arbery, Breonna Taylor, and George Floyd, even amid a global pandemic. This is a pattern rooted in systemic inequality that needs to be disrupted and dismantled.

Dialogue

Years after he called the police on the police, Mike-Mike wondered what would have happened if he had accepted the officer's request to dialogue. Could the voice of a teenager shatter the intricate power dynamics that had existed for centuries between law enforcers and marginalized youth? Would the officer have heard Mike-Mike's fear, pain, and genuineness? Could Mike-Mike have found the words? Would the officer's heart have grown two sizes bigger as he realized he was perpetuating a centuries-old system of oppressing vulnerable communities? Would Mike-Mike have heard the officer's perspective? Would he have been able to trust the officer's words, or would the screaming nightmares of a cop caging his father have drowned out the sound of his voice? Could the officer have found the words? Would Mike-Mike's anger have shrunk as he experienced his own epiphany about how the police officer was employing the only tools he was trained to use in order to be a good policeman? Would they have both realized they were pawns in a system that was not built to serve either of them? Would they have realized that their identities were both shaped by internalizing racism, classism, hypermasculinity, American capitalism, and social stratification? Would they have become brothers?

Would the policeman have leveraged his White privilege, power, and intellect to silence the voice of the oppressed and manipulated Mike-Mike into thinking his experiences were imaginary, engineered by media and disgruntled community members? Would he have succeeded in brainwashing the child and converting him into an agent of the system? Could the officer truly have had Mike-Mike's best interests at heart, or would opening up to the police have put Mike-Mike at further risk of violence and punishment? Would their dialogue have been liberating or incarcerating? Could Takers learn to become protectors? Long before Dr. Micah E. Johnson was a college professor, expert in forensic sociology, and coauthor of this book, he was Mike-Mike.

There was a time in the not-too-distant past that Jeffrey Weisberg also held preconceived notions about police officers. But in 2012, he was invited to attend a training with police officers and other state employees on a relatively new approach of bringing police and youth together in a circle to talk. As a result of that training, the River Phoenix Center for Peacebuilding (RPCP) partnered with the local police department to design a unique version of the Police Youth Dialogues with the aim of interrupting the school-to-prison pipeline and addressing the disproportionate minority contact that affects outcomes for Black and Brown youth entering the criminal justice system.

* * *

Over the past eight years, RPCP has conducted over 100 Police Youth Dialogues with 1,200 officers and 2,000 youth coming together to get real, share concerns and perceptions of each other, and begin to peel back the layers of mistrust to reveal a common humanity. At the very first dialogue that was held, youth were invited to come up with meaningful questions to ask the cops. One boy asked, "What was the most challenging thing you've ever overcome?" The first officer to respond shared that one day, her father, who was driving the car, was beating her mother in the front seat and stopped the car, kicked the family out of the car, and drove off. Another officer shared that he was sexually molested as a child. A third officer confided that his younger brother accidentally shot and killed his other brother. Everyone was rendered speechless, and youth participants began seeing the officers as people beyond the badges and guns.

Silence is the enemy of integrity. When voices exchange that are informed, respectful, and have equal authority, the voices become a chorus of truth and justice. It is in the best interest of justice, public health, and global sustainability to build peaceful connections between the law and the communities that have been historically marginalized and victimized by an unjust system. A critical step in building toward healing is to facilitate informed, respectful, and equitable dialogue between police and youth.

When voices exchange that are informed, respectful, and have equal authority, the voices become a chorus of truth and justice.

We propose Police Youth Dialogues (PYDs) as a powerful mechanism within a constellation of services that can be leveraged to address long-standing issues in policing and change the perceptions, policies, and practices of policing. If implemented regularly, PYDs may even prevent further incidents of violence. Police Youth Dialogue programs consist of a structured forum in which law enforcement officers and youth of color come together to discuss issues and concerns relevant to their community. At their core, PYDs build relationships and trust between officers and youth, promote reflection and mutual understanding of concerns related to tensions between police and youth, deconstruct biases, empower marginalized youth, allow police to keep apprised of community needs, and reenvision the role and culture of policing. Effective PYDs require best practices, thoughtful design, socially informed facilitation, and attention to potential potholes if they are to achieve these objectives, empower historically marginalized youth, and disrupt long-standing power dynamics and inequalities.

Who are considered marginalized youth? Minors and young adults who are from racial/ethnic minority backgrounds, underserved communities, and other populations relegated to the margins of society. Black and Latinx youth have a particularly fraught history with law enforcement that is most visible today, but individuals who are young women, LGBTQIA+ people, people with disabilities, immigrants, and refugees, or anyone at the intersection of these and other marginalized identities are included in our definition. Each of these groups has a unique history with the law that has hindered the cause of peace.

The purpose of this book is to honestly confront the harms committed by agents of authority and state power against marginalized groups throughout history, understand how this legacy of trauma continues to produce concentrated disadvantage and inequalities in policing practices and the criminal justice system, and explore how honest and open dialogue can help build trust between police and youth today. This book is for anyone who is interested in learning more about the fraught relationships between police and marginalized communities and who is passionate about taking action to build stronger police-community relations. Our hope is that everyone invested in the work of social justice, equity, and public safety can gain some insight from this book. Police officers may better understand the youth they serve and the complexities of their profession within the context of systemic racism and historical trauma. Community organizers may learn to implement, facilitate, or troubleshoot PYDs in their neighborhoods. Marginalized youth who are inspired to mobilize against police brutality may gain the knowledge and confidence to speak about their own experiences in community forums, police training workshops, or dialogue settings, and even become local leaders on the issue.

This book begins in the past and leads into PYDs as an actionable tool to address police violence and other police-community issues. Chapter 2 contextualizes the relationship between authority figures and marginalized communities throughout American history, from the transatlantic slave trade to police-assisted lynchings and a criminal justice system that victimize youth in marginalized communities. We trace the way state-sanctioned brutality has been enacted in defense of ideologies that privilege White, heterosexual, cisgender, able-bodied men, and oppress other groups. Chapter 3 covers the contemporary context of tensions between police and youth, including recent publicized police killings of young minority men and women without accountability, social movements and mobilization in response to these killings, disproportionate minority contact with law enforcement, and the impact of a global pandemic on policing marginalized communities. Chapter 4 focuses on the experiences of police officers, police power, and the role of policing in a larger societal context and current reform efforts. In chapter 5, we discuss PYD foundation in dialogue and the impact meaningful communication can have in empowering individuals, centering marginalized voices, and building trust and what those mean for the objectives of PYDs. In chapter 6, we feature a variety of PYD models and explore how to structure and facilitate dialogue to meet objectives. Chapter 7 addresses potential dialogue pitfalls and provides strategies for navigating them. And finally, in chapter 8, we discuss how PYD may be applied to other populations in order to foster sustainable peace and the potential impact and meaning of PYD in current calls for reform.

2
Historical Context of Policing

The relationship between law enforcement officers and the communities within which they operate are shaped by historical events, conditions, and traditions. Embracing the historical context is essential to achieving justice and stronger communities as even the most egregious atrocities can be transformed into opportunities to strengthen communities. Those interested in rebuilding and reimagining police-community relations can leverage this historical context to inform their practice, empower communities, and heal historical harms. This chapter presents the historical relationship between agents of the state and vulnerable populations, from the transatlantic slave trade and colonization to the objectification of women and the criminalization of sexual orientation. We provide an overview of the foundation of policing in this country, the enforcement of discriminatory and dehumanizing laws and practices by police, and how minority communities have been impacted.

Black Communities

> *But you are a Black boy, and you must be responsible for your body in a way that other boys cannot know. Indeed, you must be responsible for the worst actions of other Black bodies, which, somehow, will always be assigned to you. And you must be responsible for the bodies of the powerful—the policeman who cracks you with a nightstick will quickly find his excuse in your furtive movements.*
>
> —Ta-Nahisi Coates, *Between the World and Me*

When Black children reach the cusp of adolescence, their parents sit them down to have "the talk," just as Ta-Nahisi Coates does in his book of essays written as a letter to his son. These children are told how to navigate interactions with police officers and enforcers of White authority so they emerge unscathed. They are told their lives are not guaranteed in those moments. For centuries, these wisdoms have been passed from generation to generation; "the talk" has been necessary and normalized in Black communities. While policing is only a piece of larger structural, historical, and systemic issues, for centuries these entities have served as the iron fist of anti-Black racism.

The relationship between law enforcement and Black populations in the United States except for incarcerated people is rooted in White supremacy, capitalism, and chattel slavery in the colonial period. The predecessor of modern law enforcement agencies were lynch mobs and slave patrols, units made up of White volunteers who used vicious tactics to uphold the institution of slavery in the early 1700s. Their primary responsibilities were to capture and return escaped slaves, crush slave rebellions, punish those who violated plantation rules, and safeguard White supremacy. Slaves were already subjected to many forms of psychological and physical violence on a daily basis by plantation owners and overseers, including rape, whipping, beating, mutilation, hanging, separation of families, deprivation of food, and other horrors. Slave patrols and lynch mobs were the enforcers of these atrocities. Young men were often more strictly patrolled because they were the most likely to rebel and fight for a better life; slave owners and slave patrols alike sought to break this spirit.

Black inferiority and White supremacy was the law of the land. Ultimately, it was the duty of all White people to safeguard the status quo, but the slave patrols and lynch mobs were the enforcers on the front lines. Those who deviated from the racial order, White and Black, were swiftly and severely punished. Even after the ratification of the 13th Amendment, legally abolishing chattel slavery in the United States, anti-Black racist ideas and traditions thrived. Slave patrol evolved into police patrols. Plantations evolved into prisons. Lynch mobs evolved into White supremacist organizations. These groups were often closely affiliated with law enforcement entities, such as the Ku Klux Klan, which terrorized, attacked, and killed Blacks and sympathetic Whites with impunity since 1865. For many Blacks, the badge and uniform was just as much associated with White supremacy as Klan robes and Confederate flags. The police were the face of Jim Crow laws. Police officers, along with affiliated organizations and civilian mobs, committed egregious acts of violence against Blacks and Whites who peacefully advocated for basic civil rights for Black people.[1] Thousands of Blacks were lynched by mobs that were often led, sanctioned, or protected by local law enforcement.[2]

Black families witnessed police officers attack peaceful Black assemblies with police dogs, fire hoses, whips, clubs, and tear gas. Young Black children watched in terror on "Bloody Sunday" as state troopers nearly beat the late John Lewis to death as he kneeled down to pray on Edmund Pettus Bridge in Selma, Alabama. Those children gave their children "the talk" and Black folklore of police brutality became reality for many Black youth and foreshadowed their lived experiences with law enforcement. From John Lewis to Rodney King, police entities across the country routinely committed acts of violence, terror, and racial profiling in Black communities. Many police enthusiastically and aggressively enforced racist policies, such as the notorious "War on Drugs" campaign that devastated the Black community—criminalizing, stigmatizing, and incarcerating Blacks for substance misuse while simultaneously funneling behavioral health resources to White communities for the same types of substance misuse. Some argue that the very existence of police is adversarial to Black progress because the initial policing institutions were created primarily to keep Blacks in a subhuman or second-class citizen status and played a key role in Black oppression throughout history. The sentiments are corroborated by critical race theory that has demonstrated how ideas about Whiteness and "Others" are embedded in the nation's founding documents and the legal system.

Latinx Communities

Though often overlooked, Latinx communities have suffered from lynchings, attacks, profiling, bullying, sexual assault, corruption, disproportionate incarceration, and other atrocities perpetrated by law enforcement entities. For example, in 1918, the Texas Rangers, state police, US soldiers, and local vigilantes massacred 15 Mexican American men and boys, as young as 15 years old, in the village of Porvenir. None of the officers involved were prosecuted. The Porvenir massacre sparked widespread folklore on police officers and the racism, hatred, and violence they are capable of showing Latinx communities. Latinx folks, particularly in the Southwest, were also lynched by police, lynch mobs, or civilian vigilantes who were led, sanctioned, or protected by local law enforcement. Certain Latinx groups have been historically subjected to unique police scrutiny and mistreatment fueled by widely held nationalist and anti-immigration sentiments. Latinx folks were targets of cruelty for speaking Spanish or expressing pride in their heritage,[3] or simply possessing certain phenotypical characteristics associated with Latinx communities.

Native Americans

Colonizing violence against Native Americans took many forms, including acts of war and genocide, the introduction and spread of diseases, forced displacement from land, and physical violence for engaging in cultural traditions and rituals. Various groups of Uniformed white men with badges were assigned to police, patrol, and enforce cruel government policies in Native American communities. Throughout the late 1800s, men, women, and children were massacred by heavily armed US soldiers. Those who were forcibly removed from their land rather than executed died from malnutrition, exhaustion, and brutal treatment. Thousands of Chicasaw, Choctaw, Seminole, Cherokee, and Creek people perished on the "Trail of Tears" as they were relocated from their homes in the southeastern regions of the country at gunpoint to reservations in Oklahoma and other western territories. Uniformed men with badges executed forced assimilation, taking Native American youth to attend the Bureau of Indian Affairs boarding schools. Uniformed men with badges enforced racist ideologies that cast Native Americans as savage, subhuman, and inferior. For many members of these communities, police officers are the modern personification of the patrolmen, soldiers, and civilian mobs who abused, tormented, and annihilated their ancestors.

Women

The justice system was not designed for women, and therefore has not provided equal protections to women compared to men. Just as the founding institutions of this nation are entrenched in concepts of race, these institutions reflect historical ideologies of gender that position men as superior to women, including patriarchy, misogyny, and hegemonic masculinity. Policing entities, though only a piece of a larger puzzle, played a critical role in perpetuating gender inequalities, specifically by enforcing or not enforcing laws, accordingly. Under English common law, for example, a woman was legally considered the possession of her husband and police actions (or lack of action) reinforced this status.

The superiority of maleness and masculinity has survived for centuries, and police culture and identity are shaped around hypermasculinity and toxic masculinity. Hypermasculinity refers to the exaggeration of male stereotypical behavior, such as an emphasis on power, aggression, sexual conquests, and physical strength. Toxic masculinity refers to traditional cultural norms associated with ideal masculinity that can be destructive to men, women, and the larger society. However, women have suffered tremendously due to this police culture and identity. Law enforcement officers have a long history of interacting with women and girls in ways that can be demoralizing, objectifying, and re-traumatizing. These exchanges can be harsher for women and girls who are minorities, poor, or belong to another relegated group. Black women, both free and enslaved, were excluded from rape laws until the 1860s and even then, rape charges brought by Black women against White men were seldom investigated by police and were largely dismissed. When women and girls, especially Blacks and other minorities, have reported crimes to police they have been met with scrutiny, apathy, harassment, shame, ridicule, and other forms of punishment. This culture of policing deterred many women from reporting crimes, especially crimes related to sexual assault. Oftentimes, women only accessed justice as the trophies of White men, when an assault toward a woman was treated as an affront to the man she belonged to. Historically, the type of sexual assault treated most seriously by the legal system and the public was when a White woman accused a Black man. However, the actions of police or civilian groups in these cases were often more about justifying cruelty toward Black men than seeking justice for women. What happened to Emmett Till represents the White supremacists' hatred of Black boys and not the value they place on womanhood.

LGBTQIA+ Communities

Sodomy laws—laws that deem certain sex acts unnatural or immoral—have been used against LGBTQIA+ individuals to criminalize their existence for centuries in Western civilization. Gay, lesbian, bisexual, and gender nonconforming individuals have historically been the target of police harassment for gathering in groups or showing affection in public. Antiquated laws that supposedly required citizens to wear at least three articles of gender-appropriate clothing were invoked to arrest LGBTQIA+ individuals.[4] Private and public institutions—including essential services like healthcare facilities—refused to serve them. Bars and other establishments welcoming to gay and queer patrons were constantly raided by the police, their customers and servers subjected to rough treatment. In March 1969, a police raid of the Dover Hotel in Los Angeles resulted in the brutal beating and death of Howard Efland by two LAPD officers who were never held accountable. Four months later, police raided a gay bar in New York, the Stonewall Inn, roughing up patrons and arresting 13 individuals, some for violating the state's gender-appropriate clothing statute. This raid prompted the Stonewall and other riots, bringing attention to police harassment and social discrimination against LGBTQIA+ individuals. In the late 20th and early 21st centuries, police were charged with enforcing laws that systematically denied gay people the ability to raise children, justified firing them from (or not hiring them for) jobs, and denied them protection from hate crimes. In addition, law enforcement institutions are marred by a culture of homophobia, making traditional police institutions grossly disqualified to serve LGBTQIA+ communities.

Other Marginalized Communities and Intersectionality

American laws and policing practices have also marginalized communities by class and socioeconomics, geographic location, religion, and immigration status. Those who occupied more than one marginalized identity were exponentially more vulnerable to negative encounters with enforcement figures. Black women, for instance, faced the double jeopardy of victimization for being Black and for being a woman. The legal system offers another example as it was largely designed to benefit upper-class groups at the expense of lower-class groups. Whites in poor, rural, frontier, Appalachian, and geographically isolated communities have not received the same legal protections and quality of policing as middle- and upper-class Whites, particularly in comparison to those in suburban and urban communities. Though they occurred at a lesser extent compared to minorities, certain poor and geographically isolated White communities have also suffered police violence, harassment, and abuse throughout history.

Conclusion

Law enforcement officers have historically been charged with enacting, reinforcing, and defending laws that were designed to harm and disenfranchise minority populations. This history is worthy of sensitivity, respect, and consideration, especially by law enforcement professionals who pledge to serve marginalized communities. Some individuals may be inclined to shy away from these histories, due to guilt, defensiveness, willful ignorance, culture shock, or fear of consequences. Yet, embracing these truths is a key precondition for the healing and bonding process that is essential to achieve peaceful community-police relationships, as they contextualize and may influence current relationships between law enforcement and the communities they serve. The Police Youth Dialogue is an avenue by which law enforcement and citizens, youth included, can begin to discuss the historical context that is unique to their communities.

3

Policing in the Age of George Floyd

Despite decades of civil rights victories, remnants of historical traumas and inequalities remain a reality for many individuals. The modern criminal justice system remains saturated with archaic concepts of race, class, and gender. Disparities exist at all levels, from initial contact with police to sentencing. The law continues to favor more-powerful groups at the expense of less-powerful groups. This chapter explores the contemporary experience of black youth and other marginalized communities at the hands of law enforcement, beginning with the current reality of the global COVID-19 pandemic and the publicized killings of unarmed men and

The modern criminal justice system remains inundated with archaic concepts of race, class, and gender.

women of color. Even with the powerful impact of COVID-19, the sickness of anti-Black racism within the criminal justice system may be the issue that defines the time.

COVID-19 and George Floyd: Reshaping Realities

> *For the most part, journalism has decided that the coronavirus and the killing of George Floyd, a forty-six-year-old Black man, in Minneapolis, are two distinct stories. That's fiction. Floyd's murder, under the knees of a white police officer—and the demonstrations in response—occurred as part of a cascade of events. There is the history of systemic racism in America, police brutality, and protest. There is the spread of Covid-19, the disease caused by the new coronavirus, and its economic effects. Floyd had worked as a security guard, alternately at a Salvation Army and a club called Conga Latin Bistro, which closed amid the mass shutdown of bars and restaurants. On Memorial Day, he walked into a corner store for a pack of cigarettes; he was arrested for trying to pay with a fake twenty-dollar bill. His punishment was death. An autopsy report later showed that Floyd had been infected by the coronavirus before he was killed. His last words were the same as those of so many Black Americans: "I can't breathe."*
>
> —Betsy Morais and Alexandra Neason, "The Story Has Got Away From Us," *Columbia Journalism Review*, June 3, 2020.

In December 2019, there was an outbreak of a novel strain of coronavirus (coronavirus disease 2019;

COVID-19). By March 2020, the World Health Organization declared the outbreak a global pandemic, and governments around the world mandated curfews, social distancing, facial covers, closures of nonessential entities, and other measures to slow the spread. The pandemic had an immediate negative impact on the global and US economy and reshaped our day-to-day realities.

As of mid-2020, growing data indicate that the coronavirus disproportionately affects communities of color, particularly black communities. Black people nationwide make up nearly 23 percent of all Covid-19 deaths despite comprising 13 percent of the total US population. Minority and disadvantaged communities have also been hit the hardest by economic challenges produced by the Covid-19 lockdown. Thousands of workers in the restaurant, hospitality, retail, and other service industries have lost their jobs or significant income. Those who have maintained their jobs at essential service businesses, such as grocery store cashiers and delivery drivers, are exposed to increased risk for contracting the virus. Roughly 24 percent of Blacks and Latinx are employed in service industries compared to 16 percent of White populations, meaning they are at increased risk for job loss and job-related virus exposure during the pandemic.

Amid economic precarity and heightened concerns about personal safety and health, marginalized communities still worry about policing. People of color are disproportionately impacted by the virus and, at the same time, are concerned that wearing protective gear on their face could expose them to racial profiling. In a tweet that has since gone viral, Aaron

Thomas wrote: "I don't feel safe wearing a handkerchief or something else that isn't clearly a protective mask. I want to stay alive, but I also want to stay alive."

Racial profiling was not the only criminal justice concern. As epidemiologists and leading scientists around the world scrambled to find an effective vaccine, US media widely publicized terrorizing encounters, some fatal, between people of color and police or citizens. On February 23, 2020, Ahmaud Arbery was fatally shot by a former police officer and his son while he was jogging through a South Georgia neighborhood. The killing was caught on video, which was made public and went viral a few months later. Many perceived this incident as a live-action depiction of a modern-day slave patrol or lynch mob, where White citizens would stalk and kill innocent, unarmed and unsuspecting Blacks in the name of civic duty. In March 2020, Breonna Taylor was shot and killed in a "no-knock" raid where officers forcibly entered her apartment (the wrong address) to serve a warrant for a narcotics investigation. On May 25, Christian Cooper, a Black man, asked a White woman, Amy Cooper (no relation), to put her dog on a leash in Central Park. When she refused, he began filming, and in response, she told him she would tell the police that "an African American man is threatening my life" and proceeded to call 911. From Emmett Till to Christian Cooper, Amy performed a long-standing practice of White men and women calling "the law" to enforce their supremacy and make an example out of a Black person.

On the same day as the Cooper interaction, George Floyd was suffocated to death by police officers as he begged for his life and cried out for his mother. Minneapolis police officer Derek Chauvin knelt on his neck for eight minutes and 46 seconds as his words, "I can't breathe" went unheeded. George Floyd's death was captured on cell phone video and circulated globally through all forms of media. There was widespread outrage. People from all around the globe poured out of their isolation and into the streets to protest and convey solidarity with the campaign for racial justice in the United States. Youth led demonstrations demanding justice for George Floyd. The Black Lives Matter movement, mantra, and campaign for racial justice in policing was unprecedentedly embraced by diverse peoples all around the world. Discussions ranged from procedural justice to defunding police departments. Many police officers expressed unprecedented levels of remorse, solidarity, accountability, and willingness to repair the harms that have been caused by historical and present-day horrendous actions in the name of policing Black people. Despite centuries of being appallingly victimized by the criminal justice system and centuries of outcries for justice, many Black people felt that for the first time in history, masses of people were sensitive to the pain, struggle, and burdens associated with the Black experience in the United States.

As much as this increased awareness has helped galvanize action for social justice, living in an age of publicized police killings is terrifying and traumatic for the communities affected. The COVID-19 pandemic has exacerbated existing disparities caused by systemic racism, at once bringing attention to the impact of historic problems and heightening their consequences. The modern-day experiences of marginalized communities with policing echo historic ones. Only now, they are contending with the pervasive threat of police violence alongside the threat of unemployment, evictions, increased risk for virus exposure, and differential treatment in the health-care system at unprecedented levels.

Policing Youth of Color

Adolescence through young adulthood is a critical developmental stage characterized by rapid biological and social maturation. The human brain is not mature until the age of 24 or 25, according to some estimates. This nuanced period includes desires for independence, which naturally leads to clashing with adults seeking to enforce their authority and control. Juveniles typically do not possess the same level of default credibility as adults and therefore, altercations or legal disputes between adolescents and older individuals may be ruled in favor of the latter. There are tensions between the older and younger generations. Youth often represent a changing and unfamiliar world to adults. In addition, youth are often stereotyped as being entitled, uninformed, shallow, apathetic, and gullible.

As youth from minority and stigmatized communities transition from childhood to adulthood, perceptions of their youth and maturity work against them. The youth and maturity of the privileged tend to act as protective factors, whereas perceptions of marginalized youth as older than they are work against them. Studies show that police officers, and society at large, habitually overestimate the age of Black and Latino youth. In particular, one study found that police overestimated the age of Black youth by 4.59 years, meaning a 13-year-old Black teenager would be perceived as an adult, while underestimating the age of White youth by one year. Research also shows a bias against Black girls, where adult participants viewed Black girls as more adult, more knowledgeable about sex, and in less need of nurturing and protection than White girls their age. In other words, both youth and perceived age serve to delegitimize the perspectives of marginalized adolescents, the consequences of which carry over into the justice system.

All of these factors create tensions between youth and adults, especially police officers, and become intensified for minority youth who are often seen and treated as the epitome of delinquency. Youth of color, and Black youth in particular, are constantly monitored in their day-to-day lives by school officials, police, and civilians in ways that can result in violence or death. In school, youth of color are suspended and expelled at much higher rates than their White peers, the first step in the school-to-prison pipeline. Outside school, they are disproportionately stopped, questioned, and arrested by police, even though they commit crime at similar rates as White youth. They are also more likely to experience humiliating, intrusive, and threatening interactions at traffic stops and coercive searches, and to be victims of malpractice, violence, and deadly use of force. These findings suggest that encounters between youth of color and law enforcement are less about a concern with community safety and more about identifying and apprehending those who "don't belong" and controlling young marginalized bodies. Black boys and girls are not only treated as "out of place" in middle-class White neighborhoods by police officers but also questioned near or in their own homes. Even wealth does not protect Black youth, as wealth in the form of nice clothes or cars is sometimes interpreted as an indicator of drug dealing, thus putting the youth at risk. Youth of color confront a multitude of other systemic factors that place them at higher risk for engagement with law enforcement, including over-policing in low-income neighborhoods, no-knock policies, stop-and-frisk policies, the war on drugs, and other discretionary policing practices, all of which perpetuate the mass incarceration of citizens of color.

Youth of color, and Black youth in particular, are constantly monitored in their day-to-day lives by school officials, police, and civilians in ways that can result in violence or death.

Civilians also police young people of color, especially Black youth. In recent years, the news has been inundated with cases of White citizens calling the police on Black people for engaging in harmless and ordinary activities, such as sleeping in a common area of her college dormitory, barbequing in a park, and asking to use the restroom at a public establishment. This citizen surveillance of Black mobility and the practice of Black scapegoating is not only committed by White individuals but also other minority groups and, at times, older Blacks. Laws and statutes permitting citizen arrests and use of force in apprehending criminal suspects increase the likelihood that Black youth will encounter violence as a consequence of racial bias. This starkly resembles the history of false or exaggerated accusations against Black youth to reinforce the boundaries of White spaces, punish them for violating racial codes, and justify their official maltreatment. These incidences of white surveillance also highlight a stark difference in police confidence. White citizens feel very comfortable calling the police and can expect to have their concerns taken seriously, even when they are baseless or fabricated. On the other hand, when Black communities call on the police for protection, officers take longer to respond and sometimes never arrive. Studies have found that the average time for police to arrive at the scene is twice as long for Black and Latino neighborhoods than it is for predominantly White neighborhoods. Police are regularly over-deployed in White communities, leaving fewer officers available to respond to emergency calls and violent crimes in Black neighborhoods. In addition, when Black individuals call the police, they are more likely to be treated as a suspect and find themselves being arrested, detained, aggressively handled, and even shot instead of provided with protection and response services.

The consequences of citizen surveillance and disproportionality during engagement with law enforcement extends into every level of the justice system, from detention and adjudication to sentencing and probation, where youth of color experience harsher treatment, including placement in adult prisons and increased sentencing for low-level drug offenses, compared to White youth. While in the system, the overestimation of the age of Black youth contributes to this harsher sentencing. As recent cases show, high school or college-age White males tried for rape are not always convicted or receive lenient sentences and are often portrayed as young men who will lose their bright futures because of a single youthful indiscretion. On the other hand, there is a trend of convicting Black adolescents of assaults they didn't commit, allowing vigilante "justice" with no repercussions for the perpetrators (i.e., George Zimmerman), and sentencing and punishing Black adolescents as if they were adults. The presumption of innocence until proven guilty is a foundational legal philosophy of this nation but over and over, it has not been applied to marginalized youth and fails to grant them the same legal protections.

Latinx youth also have tense encounters with border patrol officers and Immigration and Customs Enforcement (ICE) with higher incidences of deportations, family separations, and travel bans—all reinforced by men wearing uniforms and badges. The militarization of the US-Mexico border has further increased violence directed toward Latino youth. In 2010, a US border patrol agent in Texas shot and killed 15-year-old Mexican national, Sergio Adrián Hernández Güereca, who was on the other side of the border in Ciudad Juárez. The Department of Justice ruled that the border patrol agent had not violated policy and no charges were ever brought against him. These events reinforce sentiments that the police are immoral, inhumane, corrupt, and dangerous.

Though the rates of police violence against Native Americans specifically are likely underestimated, Native Americans are also at an increased risk of violence and being killed during encounters with police or police-affiliated vigilantes. For example, a police officer tased an eight-year old Rosebud Sioux girl in 2013 and killed 14-year old Jason Pero on the Bad River reservation in 2017. Native Americans continue to confront police violence during protests in defense of their land and their sovereign rights, such as the protest against the Dakota Access pipeline on the Standing Rock reservation. Officers used water cannons and other aggressive tactics that resulted in serious injuries of over 200 peaceful protestors and mass arrests. While Native Americans have retained their sovereignty on tribal lands, 70 percent of them are still subject to the authority of local police and sheriff departments. In addition, tribal courts do not have the power to prosecute anyone who is not a tribal member.[1] This makes it extremely difficult for there to be appropriate accountability for police violence and misconduct toward Native Americans. The lack of resources in the reservation system, which contributes to high rates of poverty, unemployment, mental illness, and drug and alcohol abuse, further places indigenous youth at risk for contact with the criminal justice system.

Policing Girls

Issues of racial profiling, discretionary policing, violent encounters with police, and mass incarceration are also still experienced today by women, particularly Black and other minority women. The relationship between women and law enforcement remains fraught with incidents of racially motivated violence and police sexual misconduct, ranging from on-duty sexual encounters, sexual harassment of crime victims and suspects, and unwarranted custodial strip searches, as well as more egregious offenses such as rape, sexual assault, and violence. Yet these experiences are rarely highlighted in popular understandings of police violence. The #SayHerName campaign has responded by advocating for a gender-inclusive approach to racial justice that includes black women's experiences in media narratives and demands around police reform. Practices like strip or body cavity searches can be particularly harmful to women and girls, especially those from marginalized communities who disproportionately suffer trauma, sexual violence, and physical abuse. Police sexual misconduct is likely to go unreported due to feelings of humiliation, fear of being discredited, or fear of retribution. Research shows that while most officers believe police sexual misconduct is committed by rogue officers and consists primarily of consensual sex while on duty and sexual favors from "groupies," the occupational culture of sexism and hyper-masculinity in police departments provides ample opportunity and little retribution for sexual discrimination, assault, and violence against women.[2] In a national study of police sexual misconduct, researchers found that the majority of the victims were girls under the age of 18.[3]

Police sexual misconduct is likely to go unreported due to feelings of humiliation, fear of being discredited, or fear of retribution.

Policing LGBTQIA+ Youth

LGBTQIA+ youth are more likely than their heteronormative and cisgender peers to experience an official sanction, including expulsion from school, being stopped and arrested by the police, and being convicted of crimes.[4] The path to justice system involvement includes a series of traumatic experiences in the form of family rejection, instability and poverty, bullying in school, and homelessness. They are overrepresented in the child welfare system as many adolescents end up in the foster care system after rejection by their families and subsequently report feeling unsafe in group or foster homes, forcing them to seek solace in the streets. Others who stay in the system are shuffled from home to home, often with abusive situations, never staying in one place long enough to build support systems or healthy emotional connections. These children then age out of the foster care system, and, by 18 years old, many are pushed into homelessness. Some LGBTQIA+ youth are turned away from homeless shelters after intake workers learn of their sexuality under claims they could have AIDS or otherwise put other youth at the shelter at risk.[5] These dire circumstances can cause youth to turn to theft, sex work, or the drug trade in order to survive on their own.

These social factors and experiences push LGBTQIA+ youth into the juvenile justice system. LGBTQIA+ youth are more frequently stopped by police for innocuous activities, such as being at a playground after dark, congregating in the street, or listening to loud music, as well as minor infractions such as marijuana possession, drinking in public, or vandalism. They are also more susceptible to police harassment, including sexual misconduct. This is a dangerous cocktail of risk factors that endanger the well-being of LGBTQIA+ youth and foster distrust of authority figures who have repeatedly failed to protect them. Through all of this, LGBTQIA+ youth continue to experience homophobic and transphobic violence, but due to negative experiences with law enforcement, they can be reluctant to report hate crimes, even when they are injured.

Other Marginalized Groups

Other social factors impact contemporary experiences of policing. Poverty, regardless of race, is a substantial predictor of arrests, detentions, use of force, and other negative interactions with police. In addition, roughly one third to one half of all victims of police violence are disabled or have a mental health condition. Disability, from deafness or blindness to neurodivergence and physical handicaps, is often interpreted as noncompliance by law enforcement, which is then used to justify an excessive use of force. In 2015, for example, Paul Castaway's mother called the police for help when her schizophrenic son was having a manic episode. In the surveillance footage, Castaway was holding a knife to his own neck when officers shot him twice in the torso. In July 2016, two San Jose police officers shot and killed a suicidal 18-year-old, Anthony Nunez, outside his own home. The officers involved in both cases were cleared of any criminal wrongdoing by the local district attorney's office. These tragedies highlight a reality for many minority communities: even when they call the police for help, they are the ones who end up targeted and criminalized.

The overlap of two or more of these marginalized identities can make an individual especially susceptible to entangled structures of oppression. Castaway and Nunez, discussed above, were Native American and Latino, respectively. As discussed earlier, women of color are subject to the disadvantages linked to both their gender and their race. Minority LGBTQIA+ youth can face criminalization and discretionary policing due to their race or their sexuality. Communities of color and concentrated disadvantage experience multiple forms of exclusion and this is especially true within the microcosm of police encounters and justice involvement.

> **These tragedies highlight a reality for many minority communities: even when they call the police for help, they are the ones who end up targeted and criminalized.**

Conclusion

The present moment presents both the potential for progress as well as the persistence of inequalities. In the fall of 2020, Kamala Harris became the first African American, the first Asian American, and only the third female vice-presidental running mate on a major political party ticket. Less than two weeks later, unarmed Jacob Blake was shot seven times in the back as he walked toward his car in front of three of his sons. Two days later, as groups protested the shooting of Blake, 17-year-old Kyle Rittenhouse, alleging to be a member of a citizen militia, shot and killed two demonstrators. Moments later, Rittenhouse walked past police officers with an assault rifle strapped across his shoulder. He made it home safely. For many, these incidents encapsulate racial disparities in policing practices and the blurred lines between law enforcement and armed white citizens—from slave patrols to modern-day militias.

Current policing practices place youth who come from marginalized communities or identities at increased risk for incarceration and injury. Once they have a criminal record, they experience consequences that further exclude them from full participation in society, impacting their employment opportunities, housing, and access to public services. These disparities make it difficult for those most affected to believe the justice system is fair, especially when they may have negative, traumatic, and dangerous personal experiences with law enforcement. Their experiences, especially for youth of color, connect to and perpetuate historical traumas and align with folklore about oppressive police officers, perpetuating a cycle of mutual distrust, anxiety, and animosity.

The George Floyd protests have globally highlighted the consequences of these practices. Long before the protests and still today, campaigns such as the Black Lives Matter movement have received backlash and harsh criticism. Counter activists tout the maxim "All Lives Matter" or "Blue Lives Matter" and seek to invalidate racial justice demonstrations and initiatives. These counterprotests dismiss the idea that marginalized communities continue to face racism, sexism, classism, homophobia, ableism, and other types of systemic discrimination in their everyday lives. The pain of these communities is too frequently perceived to be exaggerated or false. When incidents of police brutality occur, official and mainstream responses often focus on the "danger" posed by the victim or claim they are isolated incidents committed by a few "bad apple" officers. This might come from an unwillingness to believe our justice system is unfair. But minimization of marginalized experiences at the institutional level only serves to deny the problem, creating further fractures between police officers and the community members they are meant to protect. The reality is that marginalized youth and communities still experience many of the same forms of violence and discrimination as their parents, grandparents, and great-grandparents.

The COVID-19 pandemic and the death of George Floyd have fundamentally transformed the modern world. The pandemic reminds us that acting exclusively as individuals preoccupied with our own self-interest will only ensure our extinction. The global outrage caused by the killing of George Floyd reminds us that we are intimately connected to the pain of other people and that anti-Black racism still permeates contemporary life. As the late John Lewis said, peoples all around the world were engaging in the "good trouble" of protesting social injustice. There is no better time for conversations between police officers and communities victimized by inequality in the justice system.

4
Guardians or Warriors?

When I first joined Teen Empowerment, I was around 14 years old. I grew up around a lot of gang violence and just a really negative lifestyle that is not anticipated for anyone as young as 13 or 14. I got a job through Teen Empowerment and the way I got the job is just through speaking my mind and being real about what I know about myself, what I know about the streets, and what I'm passionate about, which is being positive and being a role model for the community. They had this plan to get the cops to sit down with the teenagers in the community and have a dialogue and I remember at the beginning I was so against it because as a young individual—and even now—some of the kids I work with today are like "f the cops, the cops are wrong. They harass people, they don't care about no one," and that's the way I thought.

But I went to these dialogues and I brought a bunch of my homies that I used to be cool with at the time. . . . The significant thing I got out of it was, it wasn't just them understanding us, it was us understanding them as people. Because we had always looked at them like, "oh they're cops." It was kind of like they were robots, like they don't have no heart, they don't have no feelings—they got nothing. They just make laws and abuse us. But I remember this conversation with a cop where he was like, "I have a wife and kids at home and at the end of the day, I got to get back to them." It changed the way I look at cops overall. Even as an adult today, I still have very traumatized feelings from how I was treated by them but I look at some cops, listen to the way they talk to me, and I think "wow, like, you guys are people too."

—John Norena, former youth participant
and current Program Coordinator,
Center for Teen Empowerment

There is a reason many youth feel like cops lack humanity and compassion—it is because they have not felt or seen it in their daily lives. This does not mean, however, that all police officers are malicious. While there certainly are bad cops, police violence is not only an issue of individual behavior but also the result of a systemic environment that has been designed to disenfranchise and dehumanize certain communities. It thrives on racism, sexism, toxic masculinity, homophobia, and xenophobia, yet refuses to recognize these roots. It's set up to criminalize the victim to justify violent police actions against them and trivialize the severity of the problem. Acknowledging that BIPOC and other marginalized Americans are disproportionately involved in the justice system and killed by police is not the same as vilifying all law enforcement officers. It is not anti-police to oppose the way racism and injustice operate and infect nearly all facets of daily life, particularly in interactions with police. In this chapter, we examine the experience of policing at the individual officer level and then the systemic level, both historically and across decades of reform. We close the chapter exploring tensions between police as "guardians" and "warriors" and contemporary calls for police reform.

Policing: The Individual Officer

> *Officers tend to own this idea that at the end of the day, they just want to go home and take their uniform off and be with their family safely. I would flip the script by saying well, don't you think that these kids want to go home at the end of the day and be safe with their families as well? It's important that cops just don't own that. Not to mention, these kids can't take off their skin at the end of the day; they wear their uniforms 24/7. It's important to have these blunt, courageous conversations and feel comfortable having them.*
>
> —Captain William Halvosa,
> Gainesville Police Department

Police officers are called when people are behaving at their worst, and it is their job to intervene, making their work stressful, demanding, and often traumatizing. Even a routine traffic stop can end in a shoot-out with multiple fatalities. According to the FBI's *Law Enforcement Officers Killed and Assaulted* dataset, there were 468 incidents where officers were assaulted or injured with knives or firearms between 2011 and 2015. In 2019, 146 officers were killed in the line of duty.[1] In a climate where anti-police sentiments run high, their job can feel even more risky. This is exacerbated by incidents specifically targeting police, like the shooting of police officers in July 2016 in Dallas, Texas, at the end of demonstrations protesting the police killings of Alton Sterling and Philando Castile. Five officers were killed and nine were injured. If division and fear continues to grow between officers and marginalized communities, more lives will be needlessly lost.

Officers also confront stigma and stereotypes, often judged by the actions of others who wear the same uniform. These stigmas can include beliefs that most officers view themselves as above the law and that the police are all killers. Negative perceptions of police and generalizations that "all cops are the same" contribute to stereotyping that can make it more difficult for officers to perform their duties. Most police officers are doing the best they can to follow protocol and uphold the law. They signed up to protect and serve, which is a duty and honor many officers take very seriously.

Negative perceptions of police and generalizations that "all cops are the same" contribute to stereotyping that can make it more difficult for officers to perform their duties.

Police work today includes preventing crime, enforcing laws, apprehending criminals, responding to emergencies, and providing support services. The way an individual officer prioritizes and carries out these responsibilities is largely influenced by their department and training as well as their personal morals, beliefs, and values. Current proposals for police reform have lawmakers, community leaders, and activists inquiring about the primary role, priorities, and responsibilities of the police officer and the most effective methods for fulfilling those responsibilities. In other words: are police protectors and public servants or enforcers? Are they guardians of community safety or warriors against danger and crime? Examining departmental policing styles can reveal how these questions are currently being answered in practice.

Police departments can have drastically different cultures and styles of policing. In a seminal and still widely cited 1968 study on police organizational behavior, James Q. Wilson identified three styles of policing: legalistic, watchman, and service. The legalistic style focuses on law enforcement and relies on formal methods like arrests and citations to respond to legal violations. They emphasize professionalism and sometimes have militaristic characteristics. The watchman style focuses on maintaining peace and operates through informal methods with wide discretion. They determine the seriousness of an offense by its immediate consequences and may overlook smaller violations of the law in favor of maintaining public order. The service style prioritizes serving the community and providing assistance. They respond according to community needs and use arrests as a last resort.

In Wilson's original study, organizational police behavior was correlated with local politics. Studies since then have shown that they correspond with rural, urban, and suburban areas. For instance, a 1995 study found that state police and highway patrol agencies follow a more legalistic style, whereas suburban police departments use a service-oriented style.[2] Rural police departments operate with a watchman style. In these smaller departments, officers are often asked to perform a variety of nontraditional police functions with little assistance or resources so they use their discretion to engage in problem-solving with community members with the overall goal of keeping the peace.

These different departmental policing styles influence individual styles through selective hiring of officers who mirror department philosophies, training new recruits according to department values, and promoting those whose performance aligns with department styles while punishing officers who deviate. Individual policing styles also develop based on personal attitudes and beliefs, professional aspirations, and views of police work. These perspectives then translate to how they perform their duties, including use of force, arrests and citations, and providing assistance.

Policing: The System

Beyond individual and local structural influences, police officers have inherited a legacy of violence against marginalized communities and a socio-legal system designed to protect White authority with ramifications that persist to this day. As seen in the previous two chapters, the outcomes and experiences of our current law enforcement system have been drastically different for BIPOC citizens than they have for white citizens; police officers protect and serve white communities while surveilling and controlling marginalized communities. We have further seen that systemic racism in policing BIPOC extends into the way White citizens call the cops on Black folks for engaging in everyday activities or the way Amy Cooper knew how to weaponize police presence against Christian Cooper simply by threatening to describe him as "a Black man." Systemic racism is a public secret:[3] People acknowledge that BIPOC citizens experience policing differently with harsher outcomes but it is somehow taboo or unacceptable that racism should be the root of the problem. This subsequently reinforces racist ideas, practices, and outcomes by focusing on individual behavior and infractions, rather than systemic racism, to justify prejudiced treatment. Police officers and departments reflect this larger societal pattern and engage in public secrecy as representatives of state authority.

People acknowledge that BIPOC citizens experience policing differently with harsher outcomes but it is somehow taboo or unacceptable that racism should be the root of the problem.

In addition, the current criminal justice system is designed to defend and protect police officers against legal repercussions. Officers hold default legitimacy and their actions are automatically upheld as righteous or justified. To a certain extent, these measures are necessary for officers to do their jobs.

Laws protecting officers from criminal prosecution for fatalities in the line of duty were constructed with the same intent behind medical liability protections for doctors in the event of side effects or injuries incurred during the course of treatment; they are meant to defend professionals acting in good faith and allow them to keep doing the important job of helping, protecting, and saving people. However, the discretionary power that comes with the uniform and badge without proper channels for accountability can lead to habits of corruption and misconduct, including persistent patterns of police brutality against BIPOC. Limitless power and anonymity without repercussions can turn a Boy Scout into a bully.

Police operate in the context of this system that has historically charged them with controlling marginalized bodies and continues to protect those who have acted violently toward marginalized communities. The system of policing has gone through decades of reform and different paradigms of policing but without addressing systemic racism, each iteration of policing practices has only reinforced racist outcomes.

From Unorganized to Organized

Police departments originally evolved from more informal volunteer groups, such as slave patrols, to officially organized and paid enforcement officers, still meant to benefit and protect those in power. Early organized police departments were engaged in enforcing order against gambling and public drunkenness, surveilling and controlling immigrants and slaves, and harassing labor organizers. Many police departments were originally formed specifically to break strikes or suppress and remove immigrant or Native American communities. By the end of the 19th century, municipal departments became entrenched in politics and corruption. They provided services to political allies while harassing and arresting political opponents. This was a time when it was not uncommon for politicians to have connections to organized crime; they ran gambling, prostitution, and drug distribution rings. In this sense, police acted as the "enforcement arm of organized crime in every big city."[4]

Professionalism and Militarization

From the 1920s to the 1970s, police professionalism and a military model of policing were implemented. Greater centralization of leadership in police departments with training in military-style discipline were meant to achieve efficacy in crime control and reduce corruption. In addition, technological and scientific advancements were emphasized in police investigations as a way of maintaining objectivity, including the use of fingerprints, toxicology, and other means of collecting evidence. However, the recommended crime control tactics, such as aggressive stop-and-frisk procedures, created resentment among minority communities and became synonymous with police repression. The emphasis on crime fighting and efficiency also did nothing to address racist and sexist hiring practices.

In the early 1990s, the Department of Defense began providing local law enforcement agencies with excess military-grade equipment, including armored vehicles, assault rifles, flashbang grenades, grenade launchers, and sniper rifles. This increased use of military equipment has also been accompanied by an expansion of military tactics, such as deployment of Special Weapons and Tactics (SWAT) teams and the use of no-knock raids. Under President Trump, law enforcement access to military equipment through the 1033 program has only expanded.

Recent articles written by police officers and policing researchers mention that law enforcement training is heavily focused on officer safety to the point where every encounter is framed as a potential threat and a moment of hesitation can cause injury or death.[5] This promotes a "shoot first and ask questions later" mentality, where the risks of making a mistake while shooting are not seen as so severe as the risks of hesitating. As many cops will say, "better be judged by twelve than carried by six." Support and protection from the court systems seem to reaffirm this message. Qualified immunity and police union contracts present legal and bureaucratic barriers to prosecuting or removing officers who have been accused of using excessive force or flagged with misconduct.[6] When accompanied by implicit racial biases, these policies and training practices serve to reproduce systemic racism and state-sanctioned violence against minority communities.

Current Policing Reform: Guardians or Warriors?

From law enforcement, I really believe our role right now is to listen. . . . Our job right now is to listen and historically, we haven't done a good job of listening. And when I say listening, I mean, we will typically go into a town hall or community meeting and let people know why we do what we do. And the reality is we need to open up our ears and listen to the community's expectations of what they want to see. And I think if we actually listened, we would be surprised or shocked at what they expected out of us. . . . My belief is that—this is the long-game, first of all—we really have to redefine the role of law enforcement, you know, what is our role? I'm not trying to unemploy police officers, but I've got to let them know what their role is. When cops say, "I'm not a social worker," I say "Well, yes, you are a social worker." And I think a lot of officers have trouble reconciling that.

—Captain William Halvosa,
Gainesville Police Department

As concerns about policing continue to arise, additional philosophies and ideas for reform have emerged. In response to protests against police violence and proposals for reform in the last decade, police departments have implemented certain recommendations, including the use of body cameras, required training on implicit bias and procedural justice, de-escalation techniques, alternatives to arrest, and community policing. While these measures have seen positive results in some communities, they still do not directly address the policies, procedures, and culture that facilitate and perpetuate systemic racism and inequalities at large.

In 2016, the Cato Institute found that even though minority communities generally have less-favorable views of police, the majority of them oppose the prospect of reducing the presence of police officers in their communities, and most Americans are sympathetic toward the danger and difficulty of policing.[7] This may have changed in light of recent demands by activists and organizations, including the founders of the Black Lives Matter movement, to defund or abolish the police, which have gained significant traction. These proposals present alternatives to law enforcement as we know it, including the reallocation of funds to community health organizations and social services in underserved communities. Some are calling for the diversion of a portion of police funds toward education, jobs, housing, health care, and mental health services that marginalized communities are often denied.

Other calls for reform include more restrictive use-of-force policies and use-of-force training, demilitarization of police, reexamining police union contracts, and Justice Department consent decrees. Changes to training and policies around use of force might include de-escalation tactics, critical thinking to assess the situation, a ban on chokeholds and strangleholds, respect for the dignity of human life, exhausting all options before shooting, and a duty to intervene when other officers use undue force. These proposed reforms specifically target the issue of police brutality, and preliminary research shows that they are effective in reducing police violence and police killings.

Some are advocating for the dissolution of police departments entirely. The Minneapolis City Council has already pledged to dismantle the police department and rethink public safety; other cities, such as New York and Los Angeles, have discussed cutting police budgets significantly. Ultimately, municipalities and local leadership will need to decide what will work best in their communities, but it is clear that the role of law enforcement needs to be reimagined.

Effective police reform should benefit both officers and the public.

Others advocate for community-oriented policing that uses community partnerships, organizational transformation, and problem solving to address the underlying conditions that give rise to public safety issues. In other words, officers should not only respond to crimes after they occur but also actively engage in identifying community problems and developing solutions to address their root causes. The tenets of community-oriented and service-oriented policing are not new or revolutionary. In fact, as we discussed earlier in this chapter, predominantly white suburban communities experience service-oriented policing, while BIPOC communities experience a legalistic style of policing in which officers are focused on identifying and apprehending people who offend.

Effective police reform should benefit both officers and the public.

Conclusion

These proposed reforms begin to answer questions about how to move from a model of policing that emphasizes waging war against people who commit crimes to one that embraces community service and protection. But beyond this, we should also reexamine policing styles and how they intersect with race and power dynamics to ensure these guardian and warrior paradigms are not perpetuating harmful ideas about race, gender, and masculinity. Police reform requires open conversation about systemic racism and how it can manifest in policing practices even when there is not overt racist intent. Only by constantly revealing and addressing the public secret of systemic racism and its effects on BIPOC can we hope to dismantle its power.

Dialogue between police and marginalized communities can be leveraged to begin rethinking the role of police as protectors, rather than soldiers. Local leadership, police of all ranks, and all school and road officers can move toward marginalized youth with a new set of skills, attitudes, and behaviors that demonstrate the guardian ethos rather than that of the warrior. Similar to the valor it takes to face physical dangers in the field, police officers are being called to listen to and face historical truths and harms that may be difficult to digest. They are tasked with being brave enough to acknowledge systemic and interpersonal issues. They are charged with having the courage to allow themselves to be changed. The call of duty for professional police officers is to engage in dialogues with community members, including youth, with the intent to heal and empower their communities. As difficult as it may seem, we have seen professional police officers from diverse backgrounds rise to the occasion, displaying a tremendous amount of honor, humility, vulnerability, accountability, sensitivity, and humanity as well as an inspiring ability to change.

5

Police Youth Dialogue: Foundations and Objectives

Our police chief, Tony Jones, received a MacArthur grant to gather data on disproportionate minority contact. When he first explained to me that African American youth were being arrested at rates higher than other groups, I didn't get it. I remember saying, "We respond to behavior, Chief. If you want us to arrest more White kids, we will." It's a very hurtful allegation to be accused of arresting youth based solely on their race. But as more and more data came in, I started to question things. We started scratching our heads like, "Why are we doing this? Is this really fair?" I began to recognize we were complicit in making these outcomes worse. Then when I really started working with some of the youth and got to see the environment and the challenges they are raised in, I just realized that they had everything against them to be successful. . . . They didn't have a chance. . . . And the other thing I really had a hard time with was when I had gone out to a detention center and saw twelve year olds and eleven year olds locked up in a jail. . . . if you have any kind of humanity, and you go out and you see that, it's like "Man, we can do better than this. We've got to do better than this." And I know we distinguish it by calling it a detention center but it's still a prison. It's a jail. There's really no difference between that jail and the big jail other than that it's occupied by youth. So that to me was just heart wrenching. I struggled with trying to figure out like, what are we really hoping to accomplish here by locking them up? Are we trying to change their behavior? And how egregious really was their behavior that we have to lock them up? That was really the impetus for me to get involved in these Police Youth Dialogues.

—Captain William Halvosa,
Gainesville Police Department

When the ecosystem of communication is fractured, like it is between community and police, we are left with broken shards of information that at best trigger trivial misunderstandings and at worst cause echo chambers to form where people only talk to others who share their perspectives and distrust those who do not. Conversations about difficult subjects can often descend into reactive arguments, responding to someone else's words with one's own ideas and opinions without actually listening.

The power of dialogue lies in being able to break through confrontational defensiveness and an "us versus them" mentality in order to collectively generate thoughtful, generous, and nuanced consideration of an issue.

Police Youth Dialogues are a communication process designed to build relationships between officers and marginalized youth as they share their past experiences and ideas about issues that impact police-community tensions, including fear of the police, racial profiling in policing, and other related topics. Police Youth Dialogues involve much more than simply inviting police and marginalized youth to talk to one another. And, they are not spaces for debating sides of an issue—e.g., when police use of force is justified—or assuming malicious intent on part of the officer or young person. They are an avenue for responding to the outcomes of the impact and legacy of institutional racism in policing and collectively questioning: How can harmful policies, practices, and culture be reformed in a way that prioritizes the well-being and safety of all citizens,

The power of dialogue lies in being able to break through confrontational defensiveness and an "us versus them" mentality in order to collectively generate thoughtful, generous, and nuanced consideration of an issue.

particularly vulnerable populations? What do those most affected by current policing practices and policies have to say? Police and youth emerge from a Police Youth Dialogue with a shared understanding of their experiences and vision for how policing can be reimagined.

This chapter covers the broader theoretical principles and practices of various dialogue processes that provide the foundation for Police Youth Dialogue programs today. We discuss the meaning and principles of dialogue, different types of dialogue and how they have been employed in conflict-resolution and restorative justice settings, how they are applicable to forging stronger relationships between police and youth, and the objectives of a Police Youth Dialogue.

Definition of Dialogue

> *You hear this all the time, like "Oh, it's just talk." At the end of the day, I would say that the talk was what people actually really wanted and still want the most of. . . . The dialogue in and of itself is so valuable, that we were building community. Before we can start to do anything to repair or change what's broken, we need to continue to build. The number one thing I think we could rally people around is normalizing dialogue as a process and a tool that our community uses to address any community issue, to ensure we are engaging in a meaningful way the voices that are impacted by the community issues at the same level as those that do the work.*
>
> —Julie Burr, Youth Violence Prevention Network

Dialogue, as it appears in most dictionaries, is defined as "conversation between two or more people." The word has its roots in the Greek *dialogos,* where *dia* means "through" and *logos* means "words, speech, or discourse." While we typically think of dialogue as synonymous with "talking," David Bohm and others have distinguished dialogue from other forms of communication by the participants' commitment to listening and willingness to engage in a never-ending process of self-revision. More recently, Lisa Schrich and David Campt define dialogue as "a communication process that aims to build relationships between people as they share experiences, ideas, and information about a common concern."[1]

As a point of clarification, it is useful to determine what dialogue is not. Dialogue is not a debate where arguments are advanced, personal perspectives and assumptions are defended, and opposing positions are critiqued with the goal of discrediting them or rendering them illogical. Dialogue is also not a negotiation where participants compromise in order to arrive at a consensus. Instead, it is an exchange based primarily in mutual respect and deep listening without judgment. Dialogues share characteristics with other forms of communication, such as debates or casual conversation, but their uniqueness lies in an openness to incorporating the truth of others into one's own perspective and ideals.

Dialogue is an exchange based primarily in mutual respect and deep listening without judgment.

Dialogue Foundations of PYD

Three central dialogic formats serve as the foundation for many Police Youth Dialogue programs today. Relationships between police and marginalized youth are plagued with many of the same issues dealt with in these dialogues, and understanding these foundations can aid in the innovation of new approaches to achieving open and respectful communication.

Bohmian Dialogue

Surprisingly, one of the most prolific texts on dialogue was written by a physicist named David Bohm in the 1970s and 1980s. He argued that any chance for real communication breaks down when the compulsion to speak and defend oneself overtakes any willingness to listen. Instead of a volley between opposing thoughts, real dialogue entails a free-flowing group conversation in which participants experience everyone's perspectives equally and without judgment, practice mutual compassion, and ultimately develop deeper connections and understanding. In Bohm's words, "In a dialogue, however, nobody is trying to win . . . there is no attempt to gain points or make your particular view prevail. Rather, when any mistake is discovered on the part of anybody, everybody gains . . . a dialogue is something more of a common participation, in which we are not playing a game against each other but with each other. In a dialogue, everybody wins."[2]

Bohmian dialogues provide a space in which thought processes, emotions, and intentions can be reflected and examined collectively and individually. Participants are invited to consider the patterns of preconceptions and prejudice that influence their opinions, thoughts, and actions, and also share these insights with others. While dialogues can happen on a range of scales, Bohmian dialogue involves a group of 20–40 people seated in a circle talking to each other. Other characteristics of Bohmian dialogues include a suspension of impulses and reactions, a duration of roughly two hours over multiple regular sessions, the presence of facilitators to aid the process of collective reflection, and subjects and topics that are meaningful to participants.

For Bohm, dialogues are a collective process in which new shared meaning is created. In a passage in his essay collection *On Dialogue*, he describes this process in the following manner: "When one person says something, the other person does not in general respond with exactly the same meaning as that seen by the first person. Rather, the meanings are only *similar* and not *identical*. Thus, when the second person replies, the first person sees a difference between what he meant to say and what the other person understood. On considering this difference, he may then be able to see something new, which is relevant both to his own views and to those of the other person. And so it can go back and forth, with the continual emergence of a new content that is common to both participants. Thus, in a dialogue, each person does not attempt to make common certain ideas or items of information that are already known to him. Rather, it may be said that the two people are making something in common, i.e., creating something new together."

Circle Process

The circle process is based on indigenous talking circles used by Native Americans to resolve conflict and harm. Traditionally, talking circles brought individuals of all ages and social groups together to learn and heal. In the 1990s, the First Nations of Canada began including non-Natives in talking circles as they sought alternatives to the mass incarceration of their people, introducing lawyers, judges, and non-Native community members to their practice.

Since then, the circle process has been widely adopted and applied in restorative justice groups and peacebuilding initiatives. Restorative justice theory views criminal behavior in relation to the harm it causes, where justice is the process of repairing this harm. It advocates for meetings between the offender and the victim in which the victim is empowered to communicate with the offender about the impact of the crime and the offender is confronted with the person they have harmed and takes responsibility for their actions with the ultimate goal of restoring relationships and strengthening communities. Restorative justice principles emphasize repair over punishment and inclusion over exclusion, and promote accountability and community support. The circle process is effective as a restorative justice tool because it provides a structured and safe space for dialogue that allows everyone a chance to speak, helps to manage and effectively communicate emotional responses, and facilitates

Restorative justice principles emphasize repair over punishment, inclusion over exclusion, and promote accountability and community support.

deep listening. A typical circle is conducted with a small group of people, generally no more than 30 individuals. As its name might suggest, the circle process involves participants sitting in a circle without a table or any obstructions between them.

Essential elements of the circle process include the use of a talking piece, an opening and closing ceremony, and establishing guidelines for the dialogue to progress in a respectful manner. The opening and closing ceremonies can range from meditation on a quote relevant to the topic at hand to artistic presentations or collective breathing exercises. They are meant to symbolize a transition from everyday life into the sacred space of the circle and place participants in the mindset of open productive conversation. The talking piece is an item that is passed around the circle in order and determines whose turn it is to speak. Only the person with the talking piece may speak to prevent interruptions and reactive communication. Traditionally, the talking piece also allowed individuals who were prohibited from speaking to each other due to social taboos to communicate and hear each other. In contemporary settings, talking pieces are particularly effective in preventing people from talking over one another when emotions run high. Facilitators, typically known as "keepers," offer basic guidelines for a productive conversation such as speaking only when you have the talking piece, passing the talking piece without speaking is perfectly okay, and personal information shared in the circle stays in the circle. Participants consent to following these guidelines and offer any guidelines of their own. This leads into rounds of discussion where a question or activity is proposed by the facilitator and the talking piece is passed around until everyone has had a chance to respond before moving onto the next question or activity.

Dialogue for Diversity, Intergroup Conflict, and Historic Harms

Several dialogue models have been leveraged in work related to diversity, intergroup conflict, and historic harm. Among the first was the model devised by Angelo John Lewis, who, in the early 1990s, applied David Bohm's work to addressing inequities and disputes involving diversity in the workplace. As a Black man, he was frequently asked to join committees regarding diversity issues, and he quickly became frustrated by the nature of their meetings. The time was spent discussing intellectual theories about identity rather than listening to each other's struggles. Lewis founded the Diversity Tables at Princeton University based on the principles of Bohmian Dialogue and eventually expanded this initiative to what are now known as "Diversity Dialogue Circles."[3] These diversity circles are open-participation discussion groups where individuals are invited to speak about their experiences of diversity involving race, gender, sexual orientation, class, disability, and age. The "golden rule" of Diversity Dialogue Circles is that participants speak from their own experience rather than from an intellectual or theoretical perspective. A facilitator asks a series of open-ended questions and invites participants to share their stories related to the topic. At the conclusion of each circle, participants debrief on the process, content, and implications of what they discussed.

Dialogue frameworks are prevalent in "bottom-up" peacebuilding efforts across the world and have been employed to address prejudice and intergroup conflict in order to build relationships, promote civic participation, and incite change. There has not been significant research done on the efficacy of intergroup dialogues but the few available studies have yielded generally positive findings.[4, 5] They are a cost-effective and impactful start to solving conflicts and relationships that have been fractured by a history of harm. Dialogues bring together the people most affected by an issue or event and provide a space to address the deeper causes of conflict/harm, acknowledge responsibility, break down assumptions and biases, empower individuals and communities, and inspire action based in mutual concern. Instead of shying away from emotional topics and conversations, these dialogue processes bring them into the open in a safe way and encourage everyone involved to become better versions of themselves to achieve a common goal: a more equitable and peaceful community.

The basic principles of conflict resolution include mutual and symmetric empowerment, democratic values, acknowledgment of emotions, and collaborative problem solving. Dialogue programs that do not intentionally seek to do otherwise can result in unintentionally reproducing unequal and harmful power relations, a risk with police youth dialogues. In a study conducted on Arab-Jewish encounter programs in Israel designed to foster cross-cultural dialogue, Mohammed Abu-Nimer argues that in the absence of appropriate conflict-resolution approaches, these dialogues succeed in improving micro-level relationships but ultimately uphold the status quo rather than changing it.[6] Dialogues that do not examine oppressive structures can essentially serve to relieve the conscience of those with power and provide space for marginalized individuals to vent without any real acknowledgment of the harm that has been enacted throughout an often historically entrenched power imbalance and leave little room for reparative or restorative efforts.

Those who wish to employ dialogues in a manner not only cognizant of structural inequalities but seek to dismantle and mend relationships that have been damaged due to a long history of oppression need to be particularly attuned to advancing tenets of conflict resolution and restorative justice. The circle process has always had healing as its primary focus. The Coming to the Table approach, also known as the Transforming Historical Harm approach, is an example of a dialogue process that focuses specifically on healing racial wounds from the legacy and aftermath of slavery. THH advances understanding the history that has influenced the endurance of racial disparities, reimagining the relationships that continue to reinforce these disparities, healing from historical trauma through reconciliation, and interrupting the intergenerational transmission of trauma through action. This approach recognizes that many acts of injustice were legal when they occurred, so the focus of dialogue should shift from "who was wrong and how they should be punished to how lingering harms are still affecting people and what can be done about it."[7]

Common Elements of Dialogue

Iterations of dialogue have been used to repair or build relationships between various groups, such as between patients and medical staff, former wards of state mental hospitals and clinicians, and religious groups with conflicting ideologies.[8] The circle process has been used with perpetrators and victims of crime, with conflict in schools,[9] and as a healthy and effective way to deal with conflict within populations including homeless youth, teenagers, and gang members.

Their versatility in dealing with asymmetric relationships and controversial issues makes them useful for Police Youth Dialogues. Ultimately, community organizers and stakeholders should decide which elements they wish to incorporate in their own models of Police Youth Dialogues. For instance, Kay Pranis has designed a Police Youth Dialogue program using the circle process, incorporating opening and closing ceremonies and the use of a talking piece. Other Police Youth Dialogues have incorporated elements and principles from Bohmian dialogues and diversity circles. While each of these three dialogic foundations offer something unique, they share common elements that are particularly relevant for Police Youth Dialogues. These characteristics are what allow the dialogue to overcome typical barriers to communication, navigate difficult and emotionally charged topics, and create a safe space for open communication.

Shared Characteristics of Dialogue:

- Absence of hierarchy
- Deep listening and mutual respect
- Suspension of judgment
- Willingness to learn from others
- Collective construction of new understandings and insights
- Facilitation that supports dialogue principles

The maintenance of these principles relies in part on the dialogue's organization, facilitation, and participant cooperation.

Dialogues are only effective in these settings if there is *an absence of hierarchy and all participants have equal standing.* In PYD, this means both police and youth are granted equal opportunities to speak, with an emphasis placed on lending ample space and legitimacy to marginalized voices, ensuring that youth voices are not silenced or invalidated. Facilitators are essential in managing the power imbalance between police and youth so that the dialogue process is not re-traumatizing, as we will discuss further in the next chapter.

Dialogues are as powerful as the people who participate in them, thus requiring participants to be willing to suspend judgment and partake in a process of self-revision. If someone is convinced that their opinion or perspective is the "correct" one, they inherently dismiss the validity of others' thoughts and experiences. This type of retreat into an echo chamber or "us versus them" mentality is precisely what blocks productive communication. Dialogue participants should come ready to *listen with respect, empathy, and nonjudgment and learn from others who have opposing worldviews.* They are open to other perspectives and *creating new shared understandings of an issue that deeply affects them,* such as police brutality and violence or disproportionate minority contact. The efficacy of dialogue may vary greatly depending on the participants and their willingness to be vulnerable and fully engaged. However, dialogues are not only for those who are already susceptible to change; they should be able to reach those who are resistant to change as well.

Facilitators play an important role in *keeping participants committed to the dialogue principles* and promoting an attitude centered around non-judgmental curiosity, humility in recognizing that one's life experiences often do not apply to others, and an openness to learning from people who are different. They provide guidance, direction, and assistance to keep participant attention on valuing each other and fostering a collaborative spirit rather than a defensive or argumentative one.

Dialogue Objectives

Adherence to dialogue principles and practices makes it possible to achieve the objectives of a Police Youth Dialogue. Dialogue objectives may vary depending on what a specific community wants to accomplish but typical objectives include:

1. **Build relationships and trust between police officers and youth**. Police and youth should get to know each other as individuals outside official encounters fraught with tension and fear. They have the opportunity to forge friendships and personal relationships that extend beyond the dialogue session, which can become social capital for future events.
2. **Generate reflection and mutual understanding of concerns related to police-youth or police-community tensions** (i.e., disproportionate minority contact, intergenerational trauma and fear of police, adolescent brain development, etc.). Police and youth should emerge from

the dialogue with a deeper understanding of the underlying factors behind conflict between law enforcement and marginalized communities.

3. **Reveal and dismantle assumptions and biases.** Police Youth Dialogues challenge participants to confront their own biases about the other group and deconstruct them.
4. **Empower marginalized youth and center their voices.** Youth participants are able to voice their opinions, emotions, and experiences about police. They are empowered to help shape community-police relationships.
5. **Allow police to keep apprised of community needs.** Police have the opportunity to listen to youth, gain insight into what the community would like to see from them, and recognize their own responsibility in better serving these citizens.
6. **Reenvision the role and culture of policing.** The culture of policing will not change overnight, but regular Police Youth Dialogues can move toward an attitude and perspective of policing that is more community-centered.

Conclusion

One of the cops was in the gang unit when I was still getting into trouble. He's currently the chief of police right now. Personally, I feel so blessed to even be cool with him. . . . When I see him, we shake hands, we dab each other up. He's like one of my friends, he's one of my boys. And having that relationship is so significant to how we live as people, how we grow up in communities. Because if you had asked me five or six years ago, would I be able to be cool with the chief of police, I would be like, hell no, I don't want to be cool with the chief of police! But like I know him personally, he has my cell phone number. And I think that's very important and it's not happening around the world enough.

—John Norena, Center for Teen Empowerment, former participant and current program coordinator

We argue that dialogue between law enforcement and marginalized communities is more urgent than ever. BIPOC youth should be able to call the police for help without fear of facing suspicion themselves, feel safe engaging in daily activities without worrying they may become victims of racially motivated violence, and expect justice when someone in their community is harmed. Open, vulnerable, and honest communication between police and youth can begin to build this trust and foster lasting interpersonal relationships. In many of the communities most affected by police violence, the bravest thing officers can do is not to lay their lives on the line, but to listen. Sometimes, the highest degree of courage is simply to say, "I'm here to listen."

6
Police Youth Dialogue Models and Organization

Fulfilling the goals of a Police Youth Dialogue is not easy and can be daunting for both organizers and participants. The premise of these dialogues is to ask members of two groups who distrust one another to listen to different perspectives, empathize with one another, imagine new possibilities for a more peaceful community, and implement what they have learned into actions and attitudes in their daily lives. Community organizers, restorative justice advocates, and racial justice activists across the nation who have hosted Police Youth Dialogues, some beginning in the early 1990s, have witnessed police and youth confide in each other and build relationships that extend beyond the confines of an organized event. This chapter provides an overview of current Police Youth Dialogue models and curricula from programs around the United States, strategies for achieving dialogue objectives, and dialogue outcomes.

Police Youth Dialogue Structure and Curriculum

Police Youth Dialogue is rooted in and continues to build on the research and programming that has come before it. Some of the earliest programs and models include the *Everyday Democracy's Dialogue to Change Program for Community-Police Engagement*, the *Pennsylvania Disproportionate Minority Contact (DMC) Youth Law Enforcement Curriculum*, and the *Connecticut Effective Police Interactions with Youth Training* program. Various organizations have also developed and published police-dialogue tool kits containing information on planning a dialogue, recruiting participants, partnering with police, training and preparing facilitators, and related topics. These include the *Guide for Improving Relationships and Public Safety through Engagement and Conversation* by the Center for Court Innovation, *Youth-Led Dialogue with Law Enforcement* by the Boys and Girls Club of America, and *Youth-Police Dialogue in Circle* resource by Kay Pranis. While sharing many commonalities, they differ in the structure of the dialogue and the curriculum covered.

Single Session or Event

Many Police Youth Dialogues have adopted a format that entails a combination of sessions where youth and police meet in separate groups and joint sessions with both police and youth together during the course of a single four- to five-hour event. The River Phoenix Center for Peacebuilding in Gainesville,

Florida, has established a robust working relationship with the local police department and sheriff's office and conducted over 100 Police Youth Dialogues with 1,200 officers and 2,000 youth participating. This program is based around seven modules delivered across five hours, typically from 4 p.m. to 9 p.m. on a weekday evening to accommodate work and school schedules. Participants include 10 to 15 officers of varying ranks and the same number of youths between the ages of 14 and 24. Some of these modules are instructional and include only the officers, and others focus specifically on relationship building through dialogue and interactions with officers and youth together. Instructional content for the officers centers on disproportionate minority contact, implicit bias, adverse childhood experiences and the impact of toxic stress, and de-escalation techniques. Dialogue modules employ icebreakers, group generated agreements, discussion questions that focus on perceptions and areas of concern, one-on-one interviews over dinner, and a role play exercise where the youth demonstrate a traffic stop.

The *Bridging the Gap: Kids and Cops Program* established by the Office of Independent Monitor in the City and County of Denver follows a similar single five-hour session but was designed for a greater number of participants and a different ratio of officers to youth. Typically, their dialogue forums are attended by 50 youth, seven police officers, and seven facilitators. Initial breakout sessions separate youth and officers. Then, in the joint sessions, youth are split into seven groups of six to eight youth with one participating officer and one facilitator. The organizers intentionally want youth to outnumber the officers in each group, so they feel empowered to speak. In addition, officers are alone with a group of youth to help them feel comfortable talking freely without worrying about the perceptions of other officers in the room.

Other police community dialogues take the form of town hall or community forums. For instance, the *2014 Days of Dialogue on Police-Community Relations in the Aftermath of Ezell Ford and Michael Brown* event hosted by the Institute for Non-Violence in Los Angeles attracted roughly 200 participants, including youth, adult community members, and police officers. Participants were split into smaller groups of a dozen individuals sitting at a table with a facilitator to guide discussions.

The benefits of a single-session dialogue are that it is generally easier to get community buy-in for a one-time commitment. On the other hand, participants may be reluctant to open up to one another during their first meeting and are less likely to build lasting relationships with others who they have only met once. These pros and cons may also need to be weighed alongside other factors such as cost and available resources or personnel.

Multiple Sessions

Police Youth Dialogues can also take place over the course of several weeks. For instance, Santa Cruz's Youth Violence Prevention Task Force and Dialogues for Change conducted a police youth dialogue pilot program where the same group of officers and youth committed to six weekly sessions to talk about policing, race, and community safety. Sessions one and two focused on icebreakers and individual relationship building, sessions three and four emphasized racism and structural racism, and sessions five and six concentrated on envisioning safe equitable communities and identifying community assets in order to achieve those visions.

Similarly, the Immigrant Family Institute (IFI) holds a program for immigrant youth of color between the ages of 10 to 14, their caregivers, and Seattle police to strengthen relationships and build trust. IFI dialogues include 15 to 18 immigrant families and 15 to 20 SPD officers who meet for weekly sessions over the course of eight weeks. Each session is focused on a particular topic, such as the role of stereotypes in police community relations, envisioning healthy families and safe communities, understanding and navigating the public school system, coping with acculturative stress, and developing support networks. The curriculum is flexible and changes with the needs of the community. For instance, they added a "know your rights" segment in reaction to the anti-immigration political climate where they educate participants on the differences between local police and federal immigration enforcement.

Dialogues Embedded in Police Training Programs

Police Youth Dialogues can also be integrated into independent police training programs and police academy training for new recruits. The Fight Crime: Invest in Kids' Police Training Institute hosts a *Connecting Youth and Communities with Law Enforcement (CYCLE)* program, an interactive training and engagement program for police officers designed to transform police interactions with youth. The CYCLE program consists of 12 hours of classroom instruction for just the officers, followed by four hours of dialogue and role-playing exercises with youth. Their curriculum covers topics such as contemporary issues in law enforcement, listening skills, implicit bias, adolescent brain development, de-escalation, trauma-informed response, and building rapport. Before the final dialogue session, participating youth also receive instruction in self de-escalation, effective interactions, implicit bias, and youth brain development. In other words, the CYCLE police training program has embedded a dialogue session with youth as a capstone or culminating experience where they can put what they have learned into practice. Local police departments have implemented similar training structures, including the Gainesville Police Department and Alachua County Sheriff's office, both in Florida.

Other organizations have implemented similar approaches, partnering with their local police academies to train new recruits. Teen Empowerment has been working toward the institutionalization of Police Youth Dialogues in police departments across Boston and New York. They have also conducted training sessions with police academy cohorts on their second day of training, where youth and recruits engage in interactive activities for two hours and then share pizza. Embedding Police Youth Dialogues in police training programs, particularly required training, can help to overcome issues with recruitment and participation (discussed in further detail in chapter 7).

Activities to Achieve Dialogue Objectives

We had a couple activities that revolve around where we grew up. So, I grew up in East Sommerville. We did this interactive, a springboard interactive called group-ups. And one of the exercises was "group up based on the city you're from or neighborhood you're from," and two or three cops went over to the section for the east side of Sommerville. And I remember thinking like "Wow, I never would expect you guys to be from East Sommerville." But then I look at myself and I'm like, "Do I expect them to think I'm from East Sommerville because of the way I act and the way I am?" And so that stood out to me a lot—just thinking about how cops can be so connected to individuals in their communities in ways we don't realize. Like as a young individual I'd walk around and be like, "Oh, that cop is so mean, he's awful, he doesn't understand the struggle" but he grew up in the same neighborhood I come from so how am I going to look at him any differently?

—John Norena, Center for Teen Empowerment Dialogue Participant

While every community decides on the unique aims of their PYDs, common objectives of Police Youth Dialogues are to build relationships and trust, dismantle preconceived biases, generate discussion about concerns and experiences related to tensions between police and youth, empower youth, allow police to keep a pulse on community needs, and collectively reenvision the role and culture of policing. All of the activities and strategies employed should be intentional in trying to achieve these goals.

Building Relationships and Trust

Trusting law enforcement is difficult for people who have had traumatic experiences not only with officers, but also the law and the criminal justice system, for generations. Typically, police officers and youth only interact during the course of official on-duty encounters, such as when officers are on patrol. Some youth only see police when they, a family member, or friend is stopped and searched, issued a citation, or arrested and taken away. While a few other police youth programs have been developed over the years, such as "coffee with a cop" or "sports with cops," Police Youth Dialogues allow police and youth to get to know each other while simultaneously discussing substantive issues. The tenets of dialogue promote honest and vulnerable communication that can engender deeper relationships, connections, and trust. Trust is difficult to build and easily shattered; it also should not be given lightly. Police Youth Dialogues provide a space where officers have the opportunity to earn the trust of those who have been repeatedly harmed by people wearing a uniform and a badge.

Police Youth Dialogues provide a space where officers have the opportunity to earn the trust of those who have been repeatedly harmed by people wearing a uniform and a badge.

Interpersonal connection and trust are often based on discovering commonalities, shared experiences or trials, and mutual respect. Therefore, activities that facilitate these things should be intentionally incorporated into the dialogue. Icebreakers or other social-bonding activities should not be minimized for their impact and ability to build trust, cooperation, and even fun. Laughter is a profound tool for breaking down walls and finding our common humanity. These might include the human knot, a trust circle, bag toss, and other exercises requiring teamwork and collaborative coordination.

Several programs intentionally have officers and youth share a meal. As an organizer of the IFI dialogues stated, "It is a symbol of fellowship and unity across all cultures."[1] It encourages casual conversation and camaraderie outside the more rigid structure of the organized activities. The River Phoenix Center for Peacebuilding places officers and youth into one-on-one pairs during dinner. Potential "interview questions" are provided, but typically the participants do not use them. Afterward, they bring the whole group back together and do a debrief where they ask the youth participants, "who had the best cop?" and then ask the officers, "who had the best kid?" Everyone raises their hands wanting to share something about their dinner partner.

Police Youth Dialogues should employ activities that increasingly get more personal and facilitate a scaffolding of trust. For example, participants may start off with an icebreaker and end in a guided discussion where they share difficult moments they have had to overcome, long-term dreams, and their motivations for doing what they do. Some activities that establish deeper understanding and trust include: group-generated agreements, opinion or experience-based activities where participants move or stand if they agree as a way to find commonalities, collectively completing a task, a meaningful questions discussion round, or art-based projects and discussions.

Generate Discussion and Understanding of Tensions between Police and Youth

Most police officers do not have the opportunity to learn and reflect about the various social factors that influence youth outcomes in the criminal justice system they are a part of. Police Youth Dialogues expose participants to this information, introduce them to people who are disproportionately affected by these issues, and allow them to discuss it.

Activities geared toward generating discussion and reflection of these issues and how to address them are usually preceded by the instructional or curriculum component of dialogue sessions where experts are brought in to provide police officers with background knowledge on disproportionate minority contact, childhood trauma, fear of police, adolescent brain development, and other related topics. Guided group discussions with prepared questions can be especially helpful. For instance, the River Phoenix Center for Peacebuilding engages officers during an officer-only session in a discussion of alternatives to arrest. The facilitators ask officers to provide examples of alternatives to arrest, how they can work with other resources in the community to help youth, and how they might use discretion to best meet the needs of the community.

Dismantle Biases

Police may have biases of young BIPOC as willfully ignorant people looking to cause trouble. They may have a tendency to assume they are drug dealers, gangsters, or petty criminals. Marginalized youth often hold views of police as murderers and racists. Due to the realities of racism in the criminal justice system, reducing or eliminating police bias against marginalized youth should be emphasized. However, revealing and deconstructing the biases of all participants creates a safe atmosphere in which to speak honestly about biases and assumptions.

A key strategy for dismantling biases is to acknowledge that everyone has biases, bring them into the open, and discuss them. In an A-to-Z exercise, police and youth each come up with a list of words they associate with the other group beginning with each letter of the alphabet. It is common that youth use "killer" for K and "racist" for R, and unpacking these perceptions can lead to conversations about why they have these biases.

A key strategy for dismantling biases is to acknowledge that everyone has biases, bring them into the open, and discuss them.

The *"Bridging the Gap: Kids and Cops" program* in Denver splits youth participants into groups and asks each group to collectively create a biography for a person in a picture they are shown. In the pictures, the same model might be posing while washing a car with baggy pants in one photo and wearing a suit and tie in another, but each group is presented with different images. The groups then complete a biography sheet with questions about the individual's name, hobby, job, age, race, and whether or not they have a history of police contact. Afterward, the groups come together to present their biographies and notice that the pictures contain the same individual.

They are confronted with their own implicit biases. The discussion then focuses on how and why they each made the decisions they made in constructing their biographies so that everyone stays reflective and there is no shame or blame.

Another part of dismantling bias lies in finding a common humanity. When police and marginalized youth are able to see each other as human individuals, they are more likely to treat each other with dignity, respect, and empathy, which will in turn decrease the likelihood of violence. This can be accomplished through activities that hone deep listening as well as the activities that build relationships and trust mentioned earlier. For example, in the fishbowl exercise, participants form an inner circle and an outer circle, each one consisting of all youth or all officers. The inner circle then discusses a topic while the outer circle observes. It is an opportunity to practice concentrated attention, learning, and empathy by only providing one group the chance to talk at a time while members of the other group listen. In the Seattle IFI program for immigrant youth, families, and officers, when it was the officers' turn in the fishbowl, they discussed some of the challenges they face on a daily basis. One officer confided to the group that he leaves the house everyday not knowing whether or not he will come home or have to take someone's life. This comment resonated across the room with parents who worry about their sons not coming home. This activity allows one group to listen to the other's anxieties, struggles, and fears and realize they often share similar feelings.[2]

Empower Youth

Youth, especially youth of color, are often disempowered and silenced when it comes to identifying and solving community problems. They are seen as uneducated, troublemaking, or naïve. The reality is they have a lot to contribute. PYD seeks to position youth as "experts" in police-community relationships. The asymmetric relationship between police and youth inherently places youth in a disadvantaged position during dialogues where they may be subject to the same dynamics of dismissal and vilification marginalized people have faced when protesting or speaking up about systemic maltreatment. Empowering youth in PYD takes intentionality on part of the organizers and facilitators to uplift their voices, validate their emotions and experiences, and create an atmosphere where reminders of status and power are reduced or eliminated.

Compared to youth, law enforcement officers tend to belong to dominant or more powerful ethnic or cultural groups and have more education and training, firearms and other military technologies, authoritarian uniforms, larger bodies, more extensive vocabularies, social and professional skills, higher economic status, perceived legal impunity, and a reputation in the mainstream social imaginary as courageous, heroic, and good. All these qualities reinforce power dynamics and may influence youth and adult facilitators, steering the dialogue in a way that validates or justifies existing

PYD seeks to position youth as "experts" in police-community relationships.

practices while dismissing community concerns. In some cases, law enforcement officers completely control the dialogue and indoctrinate the youth and facilitators with their worldview. In less overt cases, the power scale subtly tips toward law enforcement but youth are equally silenced, disempowered, and invalidated. Many youths from marginalized communities arrive at these gatherings less inclined to share their perspectives due to concerns related to confrontation, safety, and being humiliated as wrong, stupid, or a bad person. Facilitators and implementers must be skillful in ensuring that these power dynamics do not corrupt the learning environment.

One way to reduce the power imbalance between police and youth is to ban the presence of the gun, badge, and uniform. Some activists posit that the presence of the gun, badge, and uniform corrupts the dialogue, since these items are intended to evoke fear, obedience, and conformity. Others propose that these symbols must be present in order to redefine their meanings in the minds of youth, to evoke feelings of safety, familiarity, and trust. The appropriate strategy will vary by context. However, to diminish the power imbalance, symbols of power should be kept minimal, but banning uniforms may not be logistically possible (i.e., the uniform, gun, and badge may be a strict requirement for all official police functions). This can be addressed by implementing strategies that employ new symbols, such as the same-shirt strategy or the 1-star-2-star method. The same-shirt strategy refers to having all participants wear the same color or identical shirts (possibly over the police officer's uniform if uniforms are required). This symbolizes equal status. Anecdotal evidence suggests that both parties quickly internalize these symbols, producing a more equitable exchange. Similarly, the 1-star-2-star T-shirt method requires participants to wear identical shirts, but law enforcement officers wear a shirt with 1 star and youth wear a shirt with 2 stars. Anecdotal evidence from facilitators indicate that once they implemented this approach, youth were more engaged and empowered, and law enforcement officers were more receptive. Other strategies include choosing a neutral community location or organizing police and youth into groups during joint sessions where youth outnumber officers.

In addition, facilitators can practice multipartiality, an approach in intergroup dialogue facilitation that focuses on balancing social power independent of and in contrast to dominant social norms in society. This means an intentional focus on affirming underrepresented perspectives and identities. Facilitators are responsible for ensuring that police do not invalidate youth experiences by correcting them or questioning their behavior as criminal as a way to justify police actions. Facilitators and officer participants both can actively validate youth by tying their experiences back to research, acknowledging their emotions, and showing them that they are not alone. Giving youth the space to cuss and speak freely, especially in sessions separate from officers, empowers youth to express themselves and allows them to process their negative perceptions and experiences of police safely.

Role-playing exercises and providing youth with leadership positions are other ways to uplift youth. Many Police Youth Dialogues include role play where the roles are reversed, and youth are acting as officers (and vice versa). In Gainesville, there are different policies about staying in the car versus having to get out of the car during a traffic stop, which has caused confusion for residents, and a role-playing exercise of this exact scenario has been used to educate youth about these different policies, providing them with knowledge of local laws. These reverse-role-play exercises also force both parties to experience a common incident in their lives from the other's position, which generates empathy.

Allow Police to Keep Apprised of Community Needs

When police departments are focused on crime rates, community voices and needs are often neglected. Police Youth Dialogues are a space where police can listen to the experiences of marginalized youth and reflect on how policing can be leveraged to help young BIPOC overcome their circumstances rather than punishing them for it.

Strategies that foster police accountability toward youth and increase interpersonal connection should be intentionally incorporated. The River Phoenix Center for Peacebuilding hosts an independent youth session followed by a joint discussion. In the youth-only session, participants identify their goals and aspirations and action steps they can take to accomplish them. Then in the joint session, they share their future dreams with the officers. Officers are asked if they have any advice or personal experience to share with youth that could help them achieve their goals.

Other activities that allow police officers to gain insight into community needs and take responsibility in serving them include discussions that explicitly ask what the community would like to see more of from officers or role-play exercises that reflect problematic and productive encounters.

Reenvision the Role and Culture of Policing

Reimagining and redefining policing at a societal level will be a long process, accompanied by departmental and legislative policy changes. Police Youth Dialogues are a viable and effective tool in this longer process and provide a concrete method for determining community needs and prioritizing them in policing. Many of the activities that help achieve the other objectives also motivate police to support BIPOC youth rather than solely serving in a punitive or disciplinary role. For instance, the discussion on alternatives to arrest mentioned earlier also helps encourage officers to rethink the role of policing. In addition, dialogues can incorporate activities or guided discussions that ask participants to collectively reenvision what policing could and should look like. In a guided discussion, facilitators might ask: What do equitable communities look like to you? What are the responsibilities and duties of police officers in these communities? Generated conversation around what's ideal and what's possible or realistic given current policies also provides participants with a broader understanding of the issues, which they can then bring into their own work and lives as police officers or community advocates.

Role of Facilitator in Dialogue:

- Clearly establish the structure and content of dialogue with participants
- Remind participants to suspend judgment of other behaviors and attitudes
- Attempt to clarify an issue from the perspective of the person speaking
- Practice multipartiality
- Ensure youth voices are not dismissed or invalidated
- Validate youth by affirming their emotions and connecting their experiences to research
- Highlight identities and perspectives that are underrepresented or not represented
- Remain attentive to participant feelings and reactions
- Invite and elicit participation from all participants
- Manage time available for dialogue
- Step in to moderate when judgments are made or experiences are invalidated

Community-Specific and Culturally Responsive Approaches

As the different models and dialogue curricula suggest, there are many ways to design and facilitate police youth dialogue. All the activities and discussion used in a Police Youth Dialogue should be tailored to the specific youth communities they are intended to serve and support.

Possible Module Topics:

- Implicit bias
- Disproportionate minority contact
- Adverse childhood experiences and the impact of toxic stress
- De-escalation techniques
- Policing, race, and community safety
- Racism and structural racism
- Envisioning safe and equitable communities
- Identifying community assets
- Role of stereotypes in police community relations
- Navigating the public school system
- Coping with acculturative stress
- Developing support networks
- "Know your rights" (for youth participants)

PYD in communities with a large population of undocumented immigrants and mixed-status families are a prime example of how dialogues should be structured around the specific problems that youth from these communities face. Organizers, facilitators, and police officer participants need to be cognizant that undocumented youth or youth with undocumented family members live in fear of the US Immigration and Customs Enforcement (ICE) and often experience constant worry that they will be forcibly separated from their loved ones by law enforcement. This can cause youth to be reluctant to report crimes and be distrustful of police officers. Therefore, breakout sessions with youth can be designed to include information about federal laws concerning noncitizens, the relationship between ICE and local authorities, and immigration proceedings so they are well-informed about their rights and can be empowered to effectively communicate with police officers. Sessions with police can focus on practices that emphasize the safety of Latinx community members regardless of citizenship status.

In addition to being community-specific, PYD requires implementing culturally responsive approaches that take the needs of diverse communities into consideration, including religious practices, cultural customs, and preferred language. If officers are working with a specific minority group, curriculum components should introduce officers to the culture and customs of that group. For instance, all baptized Sikhs carry a small ceremonial knife called a kirpan, a mandatory article of the Sikh faith. It is important for officers to learn about this, particularly if there is a Sikh community within their jurisdiction so that community members are not mistakenly arrested or charged for demonstrating their faith.

At least one facilitator should be a person of color, especially when working with minority youth. Organizers should make every effort to include and integrate BIPOC in conversations around police-community tensions and police violence, including pivotal roles in the process like that of the facilitator. Programs should mentor facilitators to be involved in the process as a way of demonstrating equity, inclusion, and empowerment. There are also a number of third-party facilitator training programs available that focus on conflict resolution or restorative justice processes that facilitators may choose to attend. In groups where participants may speak English as a second language or not at all, a translator should be provided.

Outcomes

A participant in Watsonville, she's a mother, a community member that was a part of the circle and her friend was organizing a community event. And she was like, "Well, why don't we try to get in touch with Saul at Watsonville PD, one of the officers in the circle, and see if Watsonville PD wants to come support the event and have them be involved." And she said, "I never would have thought of that before this experience nor would I have thought that I could reach out and talk to him." And it seems small, but I got goosebumps when she told me because that's a connection that didn't exist before. And so I think there's a lot of good that comes out of those individual connections and the way we show up differently in how we talk to our loved ones, to our colleagues, to other community members about what we learned in that experience, what we learned from each other, and where that goes from there. Hopefully, shifting the culture of law enforcement in some way and also shifting the culture of our society to want to work together, to feel they have a voice in public safety.

—Julie Burr, Santa Fe Violence Prevention Network Coordinator

Police Youth Dialogues have the capacity to impact police officers and youth at a personal level and create meaningful institutional change at the community level. Research on Police Youth Dialogues has included analyzing participant conversation to discern underlying causes of police youth conflict and ways to improve communication.[3] Studies show that Police Youth Dialogues improve youth and police attitudes and perceptions of one another.[4, 5] Many organizations themselves also cite a marked change in perceptions of the other group between their pre-dialogue surveys and post-dialogue surveys. YW Boston found that after their dialogues, youth reported increased comfort in talking to police, an increased sense of safety in having police in their neighborhoods, and greater willingness to report a crime. Similarly, police officers reported increased consciousness of racial dynamics, a greater effort to interact with youth outside conflict settings, and a will to incorporate learning from the dialogue into their policing practices.[6] However, additional studies are necessary to evaluate the long-term efficacy of Police Youth Dialogues and their impact in the larger community.

Police Youth Dialogues encourage difficult conversations around transparency and accountability and different issues that come up between police, community members, and young people. The ripple effects of this can be far-reaching. They can help marginalized communities build social capital and when normalized as a community building tool, enough relationships will exist to where conflict between police and BIPOC youth can be more productively defused and resolved without escalation to violence. Some dialogues have already led to changes, such as policy revisions or departmental embrace of de-escalation techniques and alternatives to arrest. The Gainesville community, for instance, has seen a 67 percent reduction in juvenile arrests and a 96 percent reduction in school arrests since first implementing the dialogues.

7
Potholes and Possible Solutions

The greatest trick of the devil, according to legend, was to convince the world that he did not exist. We cannot be tricked into thinking that injustice no longer exists and that Police Youth Dialogues will be immune to social forces that perpetuate social inequities. Injustice endures, despite extraordinary advances in technology, information, communication, moral understandings, and civil rights. Even in our language and when in dialogue, we can perpetuate oppressive ideas. Police Youth Dialogues, however, can be a catalyst of edification, justice, and peacebuilding if organizers and facilitators appropriately identify the ways in which unjust, inequitable, and oppressive forces show up in the dialogues and address them. In this chapter, we address the potholes that can contaminate dialogues and provide possible solutions. These issues can produce ineffective results, further perpetuating social inequalities.

These threats to dialogue can occur at the individual and organizational level.

Individual Level

> *When you get a bunch of cops together, they all have their own reputations and images. They want to maintain those . . . They don't want to capitulate to this sort of "hug-a-thug" training. But the kids have the same thing as well. When the kids meet before the cops come into the room, the kids hate the police and we're all racists and killers, and it's really a competition amongst themselves about who can say the meanest thing and nastiest thing about cops.*
>
> —Captain William Halvosa,
> Gainesville Police Department

Personal Biases and the Reproduction of Societal Inequalities in Interpersonal Relations

Individual or interpersonal threats to dialogue are numerous, e.g., bigotry, racism, classism, stereotypes, xenophobia, homophobia, transphobia, implicit bias, language barriers, hypermasculinity, cultural and gender insensitivity, and personality-related challenges. These biases are more likely to manifest in dynamics reproducing dominant social relations, such as the dismissal or minimization of marginalized perspectives (e.g., officers toward youth, men/boys toward women/girls) than in explicitly offensive, disrespectful, or hateful speech toward other participants. However, dialogue should be facilitated and moderated with both in mind.

The perceived "neutrality" of a color-blind approach, based on the idea that "kids and cops just don't understand each other" without addressing larger issues, can create the space for rampant microaggressions where police minimize the experiences of the youth and reinforce the legitimacy of harmful practices. For example, a Black teenager may recount a story about being followed by an officer on the way to the grocery store and subsequently detained and searched without cause. Officers might respond with, "What were you doing with your hands?" or "Maybe you matched the description of someone they were looking for." These responses fail to recognize deeper systemic inequalities and instead imply that the person who shared their story must have been doing something wrong, which only serves to reproduce interpersonal prejudice and silence BIPOC youth.

Facilitators should be conscious of when these dynamics occur and have mechanisms in place to validate BIPOC experiences. They can redirect attention from "whose fault it was" to "how were people impacted" and connect these experiences to systemic issues and research. This is also an inherent part of navigating power dynamics and ensuring marginalized voices are heard.

In addition, the reproduction of institutional inequalities at the interpersonal level can be avoided or managed with the explicit discussion of topics like the intersection of systemic racism and policing. Facilitators can leverage person-centered approaches to develop programs that accommodate the diverse needs of youth and police officers and carefully monitor for ways in which these dynamics may emerge. Facilitators may find themselves continually challenging all participants to disengage their biases, preconceptions, loyalties, and any other characteristics that will hinder their ability to be receptive to others' experiences.

Negative Attitudes and Apathy

Not everyone comes to dialogue with positive intentions or attitudes. Some officers and youth participants may bring negative attitudes and harsh criticisms while others may be nihilistic, stubborn, apathetic, or resistant to full or even partial participation. Intentionally disruptive or uncooperative attitudes can create a vortex of divisiveness, criticism, and defensiveness that blocks open and empathetic communication.

Positive intentions and attitudes may not be necessary for effectiveness as those with such a demeanor can still be positively impacted by the dialogue. Moreover, the persons who are in the greatest need of the intervention may have the least amount of enthusiasm to engage. Implementers should welcome apathetic participants. Dialogue has the power to bring people along a continuum of support, from active opposition to figuring out how they can begin to contribute. This is where the magic happens. This is particularly true when strength-based approaches are implemented to build on commonalities and similarities between police and youth to foster togetherness. Strength-based practices focus on the skills, interests, and support systems of a person or group, emphasizing their existing strengths and resources to encourage developing them further. These practices can help participants recognize each other's strengths as well as reinforcing individual self-confidence and their ability to make a difference.

In the process of recruitment, dialogue organizers may initially target low-hanging fruit, e.g., openly enthusiastic and gracious police officers, to work out the kinks and pilot test dialogues before implementing them comprehensively in the community. However, programs that are characterized by participant selection bias or that cherry-pick "friendlies" may not substantively contribute to community peacebuilding because they do not reach the people who most need the dialogue or who can implement systemic change. Implementers do well to ensure that dialogues are not entirely comprised of gracious participants, police-affiliated youth groups, or officers with administrative ambitions. If a dialogue is composed of those who are already invested in community policing or those who do not acknowledge that there is a policing issue, it is difficult to have productive conversations around community-police tensions and how to improve these relationships. Randomly selecting participants, which would ensure a mix of attitudes, may not be feasible or appropriate in certain contexts. But in general, intentionally inviting gracious participants and mixing them with more hostile participants will create a balance that may maximize effectiveness.

Strength-based practices focus on the skills, interests, and support systems of a person or group, emphasizing their existing strengths and resources to encourage developing them further.

Risk of Backlash

Participants may perceive a risk of punishment and backlash for participation in these dialogues. For example, participants may be subject to reprimand for honestly disclosing their opinions and experiences. Community activists may be reluctant to adopt a dialogue with police due to concerns over losing credibility in the community and facing accusations of pandering to power. Similarly, officers may be reluctant to engage because they fear that everything they say will be reported to their superiors.

Developing dialogue programs that have community buy-in and involvement will diminish such backlash. It is thus imperative that program developers collaborate with partnering organizations' leaders—be they police departments, youth organizations, or other community organizations—to foster a culture of mutual confidentiality and professional immunity to the extent possible. Organizers can establish ground rules or agreements to ensure that what is shared during the dialogue remains private and stays among those who participated unless they grant specific permission otherwise.

Organizational Level

> *We had trouble recruiting participants. . . . There was fear. We were going out and saying we are going to bring police and young people and community members together to talk about race and policing. And, you know, there was a lot of trepidation around, like, "Is this the police trying to feed us their agenda?" "Are the police being set up to just be ambushed in terms of anti-police rhetoric?" "What are we doing here?" We have made a lot of progress in Santa Cruz County in talking about race and*

racial inequity, and it's still really difficult and scary. So, getting people to sign up was like . . . you would tell them what it was, and they'd be like, '"But what are we doing?" So, the messaging was really a struggle. We have a dozen versions of recruitment flyers. The way we addressed it was, we tapped into our network of providers and the partners that were at the table to organize and said, "Can you please reach out to the youth and families you serve, the people in your neighborhood? Really just be a champion for this and try and get the word out."

—Julie Burr, Santa Fe Violence Prevention Network

Timing of Dialogue

Fatal police encounters and other police-community catastrophes often inspire the start of a police youth dialogue program. While understandable, this timing is not ideal because the dialogues may be emotionally charged, highly contentious, patronizing, and damaging to long-term relationships. In a moment of trauma, emotions are especially raw, and those affected are likely most concerned about surviving and getting through it rather than confronting, processing, or discussing it with police officers. Only hosting Police Youth Dialogues after a high-profile and fatal incident of police violence may also give the impression that leadership is merely using dialogue as a tool to make it appear as if they are responding or that they only care about addressing issues of policing when there is political pressure to do so. Neither of these reactions generate trust or build toward lasting change.

A more effective response is to offer dialogues routinely and consistently to build long-term relationships, especially before such incidents occur. If facilitated after a publicized police killing, the dialogue should be more focused on community building than responding to a specific tragedy. Facilitators can help keep this focus by clearly communicating the purpose and parameters of the dialogue to diminish emotionally charged exchanges and be ready to assist with communication if it becomes destructive. Overall, the community benefits most when dialogue organizers create sustainable programs, and try to avoid one-time or sporadic events in response to trending calamities.

Evaluation

There is a growing body of literature on the effectiveness of police youth dialogue, positive and negative outcomes, and risks to implementation and participation. The overwhelming majority of dialogue programs, however, have not been externally evaluated for effectiveness and do not align with an evidence-based model. Many dialogue programs are adaptations of other programs associated with positive outcomes that have been found through scientific methods. Adaptations may relate to the length of time that participants engage in dialogue at one session and over time, quality of the dialogue process and facilitation, and participant responsiveness. These adaptations lower implementation fidelity (the degree to which a program is delivered as intended by the program developers) and may not produce the desired outcomes. While the flexibility and adaptability of Police Youth Dialogues allows for the necessary community and culturally relevant adjustments, these changes may alter outcomes. It is subsequently essential for organizers to gauge the effectiveness of their local program. Evidence of effectiveness is also attractive to public and private funders who may be interested in funding the program.

Developing an evidence-based program takes time, resources, and scientific expertise and an investment in maintaining data, monitoring fidelity, and developing evidence of effectiveness. This can be achieved through partnerships with researchers at local universities, particularly those with training in implementation science and/or program evaluation in the fields of criminology, sociology, anthropology, public health, behavioral sciences, and related fields. Credentialed academics typically require some degree of compensation. However, their time may be covered by their research effort allocated by the university. Senior-level graduate students are also a great option. A literature review and program evaluation would be an excellent dissertation project for students interested in these topics. Through this type of collaboration, program developers can work with implementation scientists to delicately negotiate adaptability and fidelity when developing the dialogue model so that it achieves the desired outcomes. Evaluators also bring expertise in determining which outcomes to track, developing a secure data and research infrastructure, maintaining accountability and fidelity to the model, and following up with participants to collect data, a particularly challenging task. This program-evaluator collaboration can also be leveraged to seek private and public funding to further develop or test the effectiveness of a dialogue program.

Leadership and Community Partnerships

Apprehensive, disingenuous, or apathetic leadership is a major threat to a dialogue program. Leaders of organizations or police departments who only participate in Police Youth Dialogues to give the perception that they are addressing the concerns of marginalized citizens will not be invested in appropriate implementation or ensuring the participation of their group members. This is likely to result in surface-level programs that are unable to achieve lasting change in the community and instead reinforce the status quo.

Programs and organizations also exist within community contexts that could adversely impact the development, implementation, and sustainability of the dialogue, e.g., social disadvantage, a polarized political climate, poor transportation infrastructure, and community tensions. Leadership that does not consider the specific community context risks the integrity and success of the program, which may further impact community, youth, and police participation and even funding prospects.

Strong, collaborative, and community-minded leadership is necessary for program success.

Police Youth Dialogues usually involve a partnership between two or more organizations—such as a police department, a nonprofit focused on social equality, or youth empowerment organizations—each with their own strengths and limitations that can impact the effectiveness of the dialogue. Potential partnerships can be evaluated for their capacity to reach resistant and diverse participants, financial resources, and social capital. Implementers should seek buy-in at the highest level of governance, such as the executive director or police chief. Mobilization and activism may be necessary to encourage, convert, or remove persons in key leadership positions. The creation of diverse community coalitions and active involvement from community leaders makes it possible to address the forms and levels of threats discussed here.

Strong, collaborative, and community-minded leadership is necessary for program success.

Conclusion

We must not fall into the trap of thinking that dialogue by its very nature is free from inequitable forces or the potential for negative outcomes. Centuries of racial framing, years of socialization, and multidimensional social inequalities cannot be resolved without a substantial investment of resources, time, and positive energy. These powerful patterns of negativity exist and are at the root of tensions between police and youth. The charge of program developers is to develop and facilitate dialogues that raise participants' awareness of these tensions and contribute to successful outcomes for all. The potential potholes discussed here can compromise the dialogue process, but the strategies offered can serve to prevent, address, or minimize their impact on the overall success of the program. It is important to remember, however, that also in existence are forces more powerful than all threats combined: compassion and understanding.

8
Not Just Another Conversation

I think about my first series of dialogues. I think we had two sessions and after the second dialogue, I got into a gang-related altercation, and the same cops that were at the dialogue were at the scene and I just . . . I felt so bad. I felt like, I don't even know, like cold-hearted because I'm sitting there with these cops last week like, "Yo, yeah, I understand how you feel about your family and your kids and you're trying to look out for us" and yet I'm out there doing some crazy ass stuff and so I look at these cops, it was like two or three of them, and . . . they were really understanding. They were like, "it's okay, we make mistakes" and you know, we got a slap on the wrist. I think after that I really started to question some things. Like in my job with Teen Empowerment, did I really mean everything I was saying if I was doing what I was doing? And I started to really change my perceptions and actions. Again, I wouldn't say it happened immediately. It's

> *a process that has to really settle with you. For me, it had to be through example, with cops pulling me over and stopping me and showing empathy. . . . You can't change the issues if you can't change the people.*
>
> —John Norena, Center for Teen Empowerment

Each time the police are caught fatally shooting an unarmed person of color, we have a national conversation. Protestors demand accountability, charges may or may not be brought against the officer(s) responsible, and finally, some may be convicted. Amber Guyger was convicted and sentenced to ten years for the murder of Botham Jean in late 2019. In the wake of national protests, Derek Chauvin and the three other officers at the scene of George Floyd's death have been charged with murder and manslaughter. The officers involved in the raid during which Breonna Taylor was killed have, to date, not been charged for the actions that led to her death.

Accountability where there was none before is progress but there is still a large gap between receiving accountability and true equity. True justice is a world where Trayvon Martin, Michael Brown, Sandra Bland, Rekia Boyd, Anthony Nunez, Pedro Villanueva, Jason Pero, Botham Jean, Ahmaud Arbery, Breonna Taylor, George Floyd, and countless other victims of chronic police violence are still alive. Justice is a world where youth feel safe walking, driving, and gathering in crowds without having to worry that they may be identified as "suspicious" and lose their life. Justice is when minority youth are humanized even when they make mistakes, when sentencing is appropriate and comparable to that received by their White peers, when they are depicted and seen as boys and girls whose lives do not deserve to be ruined by misguided actions rather than criminals. Justice is when they feel equally protected rather than threatened by officers of the law.

As we write this, communities are grieving, angry, and exhausted at having to see yet another Black citizen killed on camera by an officer of the law. Even as they are trying to stay safe from a contagious, deadly virus that is disproportionately infecting and killing their communities, even as they are struggling to stay afloat in an economic crisis, people of color still have to worry about police brutality and racially motivated violence. Officers and police chiefs across the nation have expressed disgust and sadness at seeing one of their own kneel on George Floyd's neck in such a nonchalant manner, apathetic to his pleas.

Amid all the devastation, we are seeing hope in acts of solidarity between officers and protestors, widespread condemnation of systemic racism and police violence, and sweeping changes across the nation. The Louisville mayor has suspended the use of "no-knock" warrants, and Confederate monuments and statues have been removed in several cities. The San Francisco District Attorney announced a resolution to prevent the hiring of officers with a history of misconduct, and the New Jersey Attorney General announced policing reforms such as licensing police officers and expanding the use of force database. A policing reform bill has been proposed in Congress. In addition to structural changes at the federal level or even municipal level efforts to reallocate funds spent on military equipment for officers into community health services, building relationships and connections between police and minority communities at a grassroots level can have a resounding impact. This is where Police Youth Dialogues can be leveraged to foster sustained, long-term commitment to redefining the role of law enforcement in our communities.

Police Youth Dialogues offer a concrete way to meaningfully address systemic racism in policing and build toward equitable communities. These dialogues empower youth to become a part of the solution by providing a platform that centers and validates their experiences rather than dismissing them. Officers are presented with information about the history of policing and statistics on disproportionate minority contact in their communities today, learn how they can better protect youth who have been victims of a legal system designed to uphold White authority, and show youth that they are more than just "takers." Officers and youth have the opportunity to share in each other's lives in a forum outside official on-duty interactions, confront historical trauma, and move toward reconciliation. How might policing change when officers know community members personally and know their names (and vice versa)? How will public safety be improved when youth know officers personally and feel comfortable reaching out to them in times of need?

Police Youth Dialogues are not only for police and youth. Restorative and social justice advocates and anyone who recognizes inequality in the justice system can become more active allies by attending facilitator trainings or organizing dialogues in their communities. Marginalized communities should not have to bear the brunt of the work associated with eradicating injustice when they face the residual consequences of living in a nation built on colonialism and White authority; it is incumbent upon everyone who cares about equality to engage in a process of self-reflection, implement anti-discriminatory practices, and utilize tools at their disposal to help move the needle in the right direction. Police Youth Dialogues are a great mechanism for activists trying to make a difference in criminal justice reform and for community leaders who want to help increase community safety.

Dialogue-based peacebuilding is about dismantling obstacles that prevent growth and development, particularly disrupting and mending relationships with an unequal power dynamic in which one party suffers while the other benefits. The same strategies and models used in Police Youth Dialogues can be translated to other domains where there is a power difference, such as teachers and students, parents and children, correctional officers and men and women who are incarcerated, and host communities and migrants or refugees. For instance, similar dialogues can be implemented between teachers or administrators and minority students in schools, especially those with high rates

Dialogue-based peacebuilding is about dismantling obstacles that prevent growth and development, particularly disrupting and mending relationships with an unequal power dynamic in which one party suffers while the other benefits.

of referrals, suspensions, expulsions, and arrests of minority youth, as a way of disrupting the school-to-prison pipeline.

The fight for racial reconciliation and healing in our nation is a lengthy and complicated journey, and these issues of systemic racism and other forms of social inequality will not be resolved in a few hours of conversation. However, Police Youth Dialogues present a tenable and effective method for engendering empathy and connection between two groups who have come into violent and fatal confrontations with each other throughout history. These programs can accompany widespread and large-scale institutional efforts to end police violence against marginalized youth, protect vulnerable populations from harm, and build communities and neighborhoods that are safe for all. When tailored to the concerns of communities on the ground, dialogue can support each city or jurisdiction in finding solutions suitable to them. Dialogues can be an effective part of a community's tool kit in facilitating public health and safety from the ground up and in an open and honest way, where participants are able to discuss difficult topics and question current practices.

A common critique of Police Youth Dialogues is that they do not actually change anything, they merely serve to make police more palatable to the community. And certainly, there is a risk that if managed improperly, Police Youth Dialogues can reaffirm the status quo. However, when executed with evidence-based practices, restorative justice principles, and anti-racist values, Police Youth Dialogues can effectively change the policy, practices, culture, and perceptions of policing. Systemic change is not possible without personal change. Systems and institutions change when people change, and people change with dialogue.

In the aftermath of George Floyd, we are hearing from sympathetic communities across the nation saying that they cannot believe this has happened again. But it is time to recognize that disbelief, shock, and outrage in reaction to publicized police violence and killings are emotions of the privileged; only those who have not experienced these atrocities for generations are unable to comprehend how they can still be happening. For Black and other marginalized communities, another incident of police brutality or racially motivated violence is not a surprise at all. It is expected; it is a potential danger they are constantly aware of and have had to defend themselves against in a thousand different ways. It is a part of the lived experience of being Black or brown in America, and it has been normal in these communities for far too long. This needs to change. Let us listen to those most affected, reimagine the role of policing, and collectively build toward more equitable communities.

Notes

Chapter 1: The Takers

1 This is a phrase used by Malcolm X in his famous "The Ballot or the Bullet" speech in 1964, where he said "We don't see any American Dream. We've experienced only the American Nightmare. We haven't benefited from America's democracy. We've only suffered from America's hypocrisy."

Chapter 2: Historical Context of Policing

1 Hadden, S. E., 2001. *Slave patrols: Law and violence in Virginia and the Carolinas*. Harvard University Press.

2 Equal Justice Initiative (2015). Lynching in America: Con-fronting the Legacy of Racial Terror. https: //lynchinginamerica.eji.org/report/

3 Delgado, R., 2009. "Law of the Noose: A History of Latino Lynching." *Harv. CR-CLL Rev.* 44: 297.

4 Scholars have found that these laws don't actually exist. In New York, masquerade laws from 1845 that forbid individuals from painting, concealing, or disguising their face in public were invoked to arrest transgender individuals even though these laws were originally intended to prevent rural farmers from dressing like Native Americans to avoid or fight off tax collectors.

Chapter 3: Policing in the Age of George Floyd

1 Koerth-Baker, M., 2016. "Police Violence Against Native Americans Goes Far Beyond Standing Rock." Five Thirty Eight.

2 Kraska, P. B., and V. E. Kappeler, 1995. "To Serve and Pursue: Exploring Police Sexual Violence Against Women." *Justice Quarterly* 12(1): 85–111.

3 Stinson, P. M., Sr., J. Liederbach, S. L. Brewer Jr., and B. E. Mathna, 2015. Police Sexual Misconduct: A National Scale Study of Arrested Officers. *Criminal Justice Policy Review* 26(7): 665–690.

4 Unjust: How the Broken Juvenile and Criminal Justice Systems Fail LGBT Youth (August, 2016). https://www.lgbtmap.org/file/lgbt-criminal-justice-youth.pdf.

5 Kristopher Sharp, April 25, 2015. "Falling Through the Cracks: My Struggles to Survive as a Homeless Youth". Huffington Post.

Chapter 4: Guardians or Warriors?

1 "Honoring Officers Killed in 2019." The Officer Down Memorial Page (ODMP), 2019. https://www.odmp.org/search/year/2019.

2 Weisheit, R. A., D. N. Falcone, and L. E. Wells (2005). *Crime and Policing in Rural and Small-Town America*. Waveland Press.

3 This term is used by anthropologist Michael Taussig to describe a certain type of societal knowledge, or "knowing what not to know" in order to reinforce the secret.

4 Potter, G. (2013). The history of policing in the United States. *Retrieved from*: https://plsonline.eku.edu/sites/plsonline.eku.edu/files/the-history-of-policing-in-us.pdf.

5 Stoughton, Seth W. "How Police Training Contributes to Avoidable Deaths." *The Atlantic*, December 12,

2014. https://www.theatlantic.com/national/archive/2014/12/police-gun-shooting-training-ferguson/383681/.

6 An investigation conducted by Reuters reveals the way qualified immunity has allowed police brutality to go unpunished: https://www.reuters.com/investigates/special-report/usa-police-immunity-scotus/

7 Ekins, E. (June 4, 2020). Policing in America: Understanding Public Attitudes Toward the Police. Results from a National Survey. Retrieved September 9, 2020, from https://www.cato.org/survey-reports/policing-america.

Chapter 5: Police Youth Dialogue: Foundations and Objectives

1 Schirch, L., and D. Campt, 2015. *The Little Book of Dialogue for Difficult Subjects: A Practical, Hands-On Guide*. Simon and Schuster.

2 Bohm, D., 2013. *On Dialogue*. Routledge.

3 Lewis, A. J., 2010. Diversity Dialogue Circles: A Strategy for Building Bridges and Nurturing Change Agents.

4 Dessel, A. and M. E. Rogge, 2008. "Evaluation of Intergroup Dialogue: A Review of the Empirical Literature." *Conflict Resolution Quarterly* 26(2): 199–238.

5 Zúñiga, X., G. Lopez, and K. A. Ford (Eds.). (2016). *Intergroup Dialogue: Engaging Difference, Social Identities and Social Justice*. Routledge.

6 Abu-Nimer, M., 2012. *Dialogue, Conflict Resolution, and Change: Arab-Jewish Encounters in Israel*. SUNY Press.

7 Hooker, D., and A. Czajkowski, 2013. Transforming Historical Harms: Coming to the Table: Eastern

Mennonite University Center for Justice and Peacebuilding.
8 Stains Jr., R.R., 2014. "Repairing the Breach: The Power of Dialogue to Heal Relationships and Communities." *Journal of Public Deliberation* 10(1): 7.
9 Bickmore, K., 2013. "Peacebuilding through Circle Dialogue Processes in Primary Classrooms." *Restorative Approaches to Conflict in Schools: Interdisciplinary Perspectives on Whole School Approaches to Managing Relationships*, p.175.

Chapter 6: Police Youth Dialogue Models and Organization

1 "Strengthening Relationships Between Police and Immigrant Communities in a Complex Political Environment: Multicultural Outreach and Engagement Programs for Police Agencies," *Executive Police Forum*, p. 32.
2 Ibid., p. 31.
3 Giwa, S., C. E. James, U. Anucha, and K. Schwartz (2014). "Community Policing—A Shared Responsibility: A Voice-Centered Relational Method Analysis of a Police/Youth of Color Dialogue." *Journal of Ethnicity in Criminal Justice* 12(3): 218–245.
4 Williams, R., and C. Crifasi (2020). "Evaluating the Impact of Baltimore Community Mediation Center's Youth-Police Dialogue Circle Program." *Injury Prevention* 26(Suppl 1): A38.
5 Flemming, P. S. (2015). Teen Empowerment's Youth/Police Dialogues: The Bridge to Improving Police and Youth Relations.
6 YW Boston Youth Police Dialogue Program Overview. Accessed at: http://www.ywboston.org/wp-content/uploads/2016/02/YW-Boston-Youth-Police-Dialogues-Program-Overview.pdf

Acknowledgments

The inception of this book was born from the belief that peace is possible and driven by the desire to grow peacebuilding practices around the globe.

At the River Phoenix Center for Peacebuilding, we saw time and time again that dialogue was key to understanding and healing conflicts and bridging divides that only grow isolation, fear, and mistrust. In 2013 we were invited by the local police department to assist in the creation of a dialogue program that would foster trust, promote understanding, and break down stereotypes between law enforcement officers and predominantly youth of color.

We are ever grateful for the courage of the countless youth who participated in the many police/youth dialogues over the past seven years. Their ability to speak their fear, pain, and challenges as they stood face to face with officers was spellbinding. We appreciate the officers who were able to share their stories, listen deeply to youth, acknowledge their own pain, and realize they cannot create safe and vibrant communities without the partnership with both youth and adults. And so, we come together in dialogue and leave having built more trust, cooperation, understanding, and mutual respect.

Our deepest gratitude goes to Police Chief Tony Jones and retired Captain Will Halvosa of the Gainesville Police Department, who have been our partners from the beginning, as well as Sergeant Paul Pardue at the Alachua County Sheriff's Office. Each of these officers have led the way in this most important work.

We are grateful for Dr. Jandy Gu for her invaluable contribution to this book as well as Dr. Barb Toews for her remarkable guidance and support. Finally, we are indebted to the activists, peacebuilders, and humanitarians who continue to invest in the well-being, equity, and moral development of our human family.

About the Authors

Jeffrey Weisberg has been a champion of change, social justice advocate, activist, and facilitator of thousands of community peacebuilding programs over the past thirty years throughout the US and abroad. He cofounded the River Phoenix Center for Peacebuilding (RPCP) in Gainesville, Florida with Heart Phoenix (who is his wife and life partner) in 2011.

His leadership and innovation in developing a Comprehensive Peacebuilding model for communities has helped expand core peace practices across the United States and in Ukraine, Australia, Norway, Bosnia and Herzegovina, Israel, Serbia, and Sierra Leone.

For the past twenty-plus years, Jeffrey has served as a Florida Certified State Mediator involving juvenile offenders, family disputes, and conflicts within small businesses and organizations.

His work at RPCP as Executive Director encompasses a wide range of programs including police/youth dialogues, student/educator dialogues, peer mediation, juvenile diversion programs, social/emotional learning, restorative justice and practices, youth empowerment, and coming-of-age programs. He is a cofounder of Peace4Gainesville, a Trauma Responsive Community Initiative that offers strategies to enhance resilience and interrupt the cycle of violence.

His solution-based approach to conflict stems from the premise that within conflict, there is great potential for change, deeper connection, and new pathways of understanding and collaboration.

Jeffrey aspires to embed best and next practices of peacebuilding within the Department of Juvenile Justice, court systems, schools, prisons, local communities, and re-entry efforts to bolster alternatives to the punitive model.

Dr. Micah E. Johnson is a sociologist trained in criminology and psychiatric epidemiology. He serves as an assistant professor in the Department of Mental Health Law and Policy at the University of South Florida. Dr. Johnson's research centers around childhood trauma, behavioral health, and juvenile justice. His research has been funded by the National Institutes of Health. He has been an advocate for social justice for the past fourteen years. Dr. Johnson trains, speaks, and teaches internationally on topics related to trauma, poverty, antiracism, and sustainable peace. He is a pioneer of applied forensic sociology. He founded Johnson Forensic Services and serves in the state and federal court system as an expert witness and facilitator. His philanthropic and research interests in these areas are fueled by his childhood experiences. Dr. Johnson also leverages his artistry as a poet, monologist, and speaker, to share his peacebuilding efforts with a broader audience. For information on his research, talks, or forensic services, contact DoctorMicahJohnson@gmail.com or visit www.DoctorMicahJohnson.com.